# Kerberos: Secure Authentication in Enterprise Networks

James Relington

# DEDICATION

To those who seek knowledge, inspiration, and new perspectives—
may this book be a companion on your journey, a spark for curiosity,
and a reminder that every page turned is a step toward discovery.

# AKNOWLEDGEMENTS

I would like to express my deepest gratitude to everyone who contributed to the creation of this book. To my colleagues and mentors, your insights and expertise have been invaluable. A special thank you to my family and friends for their unwavering support and encouragement throughout this journey.

# Introduction to Kerberos

In modern enterprise networks, the need for secure and efficient authentication protocols has never been more critical. As organizations grow and their IT infrastructures expand, the challenge of maintaining robust security while ensuring seamless user access becomes increasingly complex. Among the various technologies developed to address this challenge, Kerberos stands out as a time-tested and widely adopted protocol that forms the foundation for secure authentication in countless enterprise environments around the world.

Kerberos is a network authentication protocol designed to provide strong authentication for client-server applications by using secret-key cryptography. Originally developed at the Massachusetts Institute of Technology (MIT) as part of Project Athena in the 1980s, Kerberos was created to tackle the pressing need for a secure means of identifying users and services over an insecure network. The name Kerberos comes from Greek mythology, referencing the three-headed dog, Cerberus, which guarded the gates of the underworld. This metaphor captures the protocol's role as a guardian, protecting network resources from unauthorized access.

The core purpose of Kerberos is to enable entities communicating over a non-secure network to prove their identity to each other in a secure manner. By doing so, it helps eliminate common security threats such as eavesdropping and replay attacks. The protocol achieves this through a ticket-based system that relies on a trusted third-party known as the Key Distribution Center, or KDC. The KDC is the backbone of any Kerberos implementation, managing the issuance and validation of tickets used for authentication. This trusted authority is responsible for holding the cryptographic keys used to verify users and services, ensuring that only legitimate parties gain access to network resources.

Unlike traditional username and password schemes, Kerberos introduces a more sophisticated approach by utilizing temporary, encrypted tickets to grant access. These tickets, known as Ticket Granting Tickets (TGTs) and service tickets, allow users to authenticate once and then securely access multiple services without re-entering their credentials. This concept, commonly referred to as Single Sign-On or SSO, enhances both security and user experience, as it reduces the likelihood of password fatigue and minimizes the risk of password-related attacks.

One of the defining features of Kerberos is its reliance on symmetric key cryptography, where the same secret key is used for both encryption and decryption. Every principal, which can be a user or a service within the network, shares a unique secret key with the KDC. This shared key forms the basis for the secure generation and validation of tickets. By leveraging strong encryption and well-defined protocols, Kerberos ensures that credentials are never transmitted in plaintext over the network, thus safeguarding sensitive information from potential attackers.

Time synchronization is another critical component in the Kerberos protocol. To mitigate the risk of replay attacks, where an attacker intercepts and reuses valid authentication data, Kerberos requires that all participating devices maintain closely synchronized clocks. Typically, the allowable time skew between clients and the KDC is limited to a few minutes. If the timestamp on a ticket falls outside this permissible window, the ticket is rejected, adding an additional layer of protection against unauthorized access.

Kerberos operates within the concept of a realm, which is the logical network boundary within which the authentication protocol is valid. A realm is typically mapped to an organization or a domain and serves as a trust domain for all Kerberos-related operations. In environments where collaboration between different organizations or domains is necessary, Kerberos supports cross-realm authentication, allowing users in one realm to access services in another through a carefully established trust relationship between KDCs.

As enterprise networks have evolved, Kerberos has demonstrated remarkable adaptability, integrating with various operating systems and technologies. It is a fundamental component of Microsoft's Active Directory, where it plays a pivotal role in authenticating users and services across Windows-based domains. Additionally, Kerberos is widely deployed in UNIX and Linux environments, where it secures access to critical services such as network file systems, databases, and web applications.

Despite its origins in academia, Kerberos has become a cornerstone of enterprise security. Its robust design and proven effectiveness in protecting sensitive data have earned it widespread adoption across industries including finance, healthcare, government, and education. Organizations rely on Kerberos not only for its technical merits but also for its ability to scale across complex, distributed environments where secure and efficient authentication is paramount.

However, like any security technology, Kerberos is not without its challenges. The protocol's dependency on time synchronization and its reliance on a centralized KDC make it susceptible to operational issues if not properly maintained. Moreover, as attackers become more sophisticated, they have developed techniques to exploit weaknesses in poorly configured Kerberos environments. Consequently, understanding the fundamental principles of Kerberos, its architecture, and its operational intricacies is essential for security professionals tasked with protecting modern enterprise networks.

Kerberos continues to be a vital part of the security landscape, evolving to meet the demands of today's hybrid and cloud-based infrastructures. While new authentication methods and technologies have emerged, Kerberos remains a key player, offering a secure, scalable, and efficient solution for authentication across diverse environments. As organizations increasingly embrace digital transformation, the importance of Kerberos and its role in safeguarding enterprise networks is more relevant than ever.

# The Evolution of Network Authentication

The journey of network authentication has been marked by continuous adaptation to the ever-changing landscape of technology and security threats. In the earliest days of computing, when systems were isolated and users interacted with a single machine in a controlled environment, authentication was a simple matter. A basic username and password were sufficient to validate a user's identity. Security was largely physical, relying on locked doors and restricted access to hardware. However, as computing moved beyond the confines of standalone machines to interconnected networks, this rudimentary approach to authentication quickly became inadequate.

With the rise of local area networks (LANs) and later wide area networks (WANs), users gained the ability to access resources across multiple systems. This shift exposed authentication protocols to new vulnerabilities, as data transmitted over untrusted networks became susceptible to interception. Passwords sent in plaintext across these networks could easily be captured by attackers using packet-sniffing tools, leading to a surge in unauthorized access incidents. This security gap highlighted the urgent need for stronger, network-aware authentication mechanisms that could protect sensitive credentials from prying eyes.

In response, early innovations in network authentication emerged during the 1970s and 1980s. One such advancement was the introduction of challenge-response protocols. Unlike plaintext password schemes, challenge-response systems added a layer of complexity by requiring users to prove knowledge of a secret without directly transmitting it. When a user attempted to authenticate, the server would issue a challenge, such as a random number or string, which the user's system would then encrypt using a shared secret key or password. The encrypted response would be sent back to the server, which would verify it against its own calculation. This technique significantly reduced the exposure of sensitive information during authentication.

As networked systems grew more sophisticated and the internet began to take shape, organizations recognized that centralized control over authentication was necessary to manage growing user populations and distributed resources. This realization gave rise to centralized authentication systems such as RADIUS (Remote Authentication Dial-In User Service) and TACACS (Terminal Access Controller Access-Control System). These protocols allowed for centralized authentication, authorization, and accounting (AAA) services, providing network administrators with greater control and visibility over user access. While RADIUS and TACACS improved the scalability and manageability of authentication, they still often relied on transmitting hashed or encrypted passwords, which, though an improvement, did not fully eliminate the risk of credential theft.

Simultaneously, the development of distributed computing environments introduced additional challenges to authentication. In distributed systems, users needed to access services spread across multiple servers without the burden of repeatedly entering their credentials. This need for efficiency and security paved the way for the concept of Single Sign-On (SSO), where users could authenticate once and gain access to a suite of services within a trusted domain. To achieve this, authentication systems began to incorporate the use of tickets or tokens, which could securely represent a user's identity across multiple sessions.

One of the landmark innovations in this era was the introduction of Kerberos in the late 1980s. Kerberos revolutionized network authentication by leveraging symmetric key cryptography and a trusted third-party model to provide secure, ticket-based authentication across untrusted networks. By issuing time-sensitive tickets encrypted with secret keys shared between users, services, and a central Key Distribution Center (KDC), Kerberos enabled mutual authentication while reducing the need to transmit reusable credentials. Kerberos' design was particularly well-suited to academic and enterprise environments, where large numbers of users required access to distributed services within a secure framework.

As internet usage proliferated in the 1990s, new challenges emerged, particularly in the realm of web-based authentication. The rise of HTTP-based applications introduced stateless communication, where each client request was independent of previous ones. This created a need for session management and user identification that went beyond the capabilities of traditional network authentication methods. In response, web developers adopted mechanisms such as HTTP basic and digest authentication, as well as cookie-based session tokens, to maintain state and verify user identities.

The late 1990s and early 2000s saw further evolution with the adoption of Public Key Infrastructure (PKI) and the use of digital certificates for authentication. By leveraging asymmetric cryptography, PKI enabled secure, certificate-based authentication, reducing reliance on shared secrets. Technologies such as SSL/TLS became integral to securing web communications, ensuring that authentication and data exchange occurred over encrypted channels. This period also marked the introduction of federated identity solutions, such as SAML (Security Assertion Markup Language), which facilitated authentication across organizational boundaries through the exchange of signed XML assertions between identity providers and service providers.

In recent years, the expansion of cloud computing, mobile access, and hybrid IT environments has driven the need for even more advanced authentication frameworks. Protocols like OAuth and OpenID Connect have gained prominence, enabling secure delegation of access rights and user authentication in cloud-native applications and APIs. Meanwhile, the rise of multi-factor authentication (MFA) has strengthened the authentication process by requiring users to present multiple forms of verification, such as passwords combined with biometrics or hardware tokens.

Despite the advances in authentication technology, legacy protocols like Kerberos continue to play a pivotal role in modern enterprises, particularly in environments that rely on on-premises infrastructure or hybrid models combining cloud and local resources. The resilience and adaptability of Kerberos, along with its integration into key systems such as Microsoft Active Directory, underscore its continued relevance.

The evolution of network authentication has been shaped by the constant interplay between technological innovation and the escalating sophistication of cyber threats. From simple password checks on isolated systems to today's complex, multi-layered authentication ecosystems, each advancement has aimed to balance security, usability, and scalability. As networks and applications grow more interconnected and attackers find new methods to exploit weaknesses, authentication protocols will undoubtedly continue to evolve, building upon the foundations established over decades of development.

# The Basics of Secure Authentication

Secure authentication is a fundamental pillar of information security, ensuring that only authorized users and systems are granted access to sensitive data and resources. At its core, authentication is the process of verifying an identity. Whether it is a user trying to log into a workstation, a server establishing communication with another server, or a device attempting to connect to a network, authentication determines whether the presented credentials are valid and trustworthy. While this concept might seem straightforward, implementing authentication securely in modern networks is a complex task, shaped by evolving technologies and the ever-present threat of cyberattacks.

The basic model of authentication involves two primary entities: a subject, which is the user or system requesting access, and an authenticator, which is the system or service validating the credentials. Traditionally, authentication relied heavily on something the user knows, most commonly a password. The subject would present a username and password, and if these matched the records stored on the authenticator's side, access would be granted. However, as networks became more interconnected and threats more sophisticated, it became clear that passwords alone could no longer provide sufficient security.

One of the core principles behind secure authentication is the protection of credentials during both storage and transmission. Insecure systems that store plaintext passwords create a massive vulnerability, as attackers who gain access to the database can immediately compromise all accounts. To mitigate this risk, secure systems employ cryptographic techniques, such as hashing, to transform passwords into irreversible values before storing them. A hash function takes an input, like a password, and produces a fixed-size output that appears random. When a user attempts to authenticate, the system hashes the provided password and compares it to the stored hash. If the hashes match, the system confirms the user's identity.

While hashing improves the security of stored passwords, protecting credentials in transit is equally important. In unprotected networks, transmitting passwords or authentication tokens without encryption exposes them to interception. Attackers equipped with packet sniffers can capture network traffic and retrieve sensitive information. To counter this, secure authentication protocols use encryption to shield communications from eavesdroppers. Technologies such as Transport Layer Security (TLS) create encrypted tunnels between clients and servers, ensuring that credentials and other sensitive data remain confidential while traversing the network.

The traditional password-based model is further enhanced through the implementation of multi-factor authentication (MFA). MFA requires users to present more than one form of verification to prove their identity, combining something they know (like a password), something they have (such as a smart card or a mobile authentication app), or something they are (such as a fingerprint or facial recognition). This layered approach significantly raises the bar for attackers, who would now need to compromise multiple independent factors to impersonate a user successfully. MFA has become a standard practice in securing access to critical systems and services, from enterprise applications to online banking platforms.

Beyond user authentication, secure authentication mechanisms are crucial for establishing trust between machines and services. Machine-to-machine authentication is a cornerstone of secure communications in distributed systems and modern applications. In these scenarios, protocols often use cryptographic keys or digital certificates to verify the identities of the communicating parties. Public Key Infrastructure (PKI) plays a critical role here, using pairs of public and private keys alongside trusted certificate authorities to authenticate systems securely. For example, during the initial handshake of an HTTPS session, a server presents its digital certificate to prove its identity to the client, which then checks the certificate against trusted authorities before proceeding with the encrypted session.

Session management is another important aspect of secure authentication. Once a user or system has been authenticated, a session is typically established to maintain state between the client and the server. This session is usually represented by a token or session ID, which is passed between the client and server with each request. Secure authentication systems ensure that session tokens are randomly generated, have a limited lifespan, and are transmitted over secure channels. Failing to properly secure session tokens can lead to session hijacking attacks, where an attacker takes over an authenticated session by stealing or guessing a valid token.

Authentication protocols are designed to balance security with usability. Complex or cumbersome authentication mechanisms can create friction for end users, potentially leading them to seek insecure workarounds. For instance, users who are frustrated by frequent password changes might resort to using weaker passwords or writing them down. Secure authentication solutions strive to provide strong protection while minimizing inconvenience, which is why single sign-on (SSO) has gained popularity. With SSO, users authenticate once and gain seamless access to multiple related systems or services without having to re-enter their credentials repeatedly. This not only improves user experience but also reduces the number of times credentials are entered and transmitted, lowering the overall risk of credential compromise.

Protocols like Kerberos, OAuth, OpenID Connect, and SAML have emerged as industry standards, each addressing specific authentication challenges. Kerberos, for instance, uses encrypted tickets to securely authenticate users in a distributed network. OAuth and OpenID Connect are widely used for authorizing third-party applications and enabling federated identity systems, particularly in web and cloud environments. SAML facilitates secure authentication across different organizations by exchanging digitally signed authentication assertions between identity providers and service providers.

Secure authentication is a dynamic and evolving discipline. Attackers continuously develop new methods to bypass or compromise authentication mechanisms, including phishing attacks, credential stuffing, and brute-force attacks. To stay ahead, organizations must adopt modern, layered authentication strategies, enforce best practices, and continually monitor authentication events for signs of malicious activity. By understanding the fundamental principles and challenges of secure authentication, organizations are better equipped to protect their assets, ensure compliance with regulations, and maintain the trust of their users and partners.

# Principles of Kerberos Protocol

The Kerberos protocol is a cornerstone of secure authentication in distributed network environments. It was specifically designed to address the security challenges associated with open networks, where sensitive data and credentials might otherwise be exposed to interception and tampering. The foundational principles of Kerberos revolve around the concepts of trusted third-party authentication, symmetric key cryptography, mutual trust, and the use of time-sensitive tickets to control access to resources.

At the heart of Kerberos is the idea of a centralized trusted authority known as the Key Distribution Center, or KDC. The KDC is responsible for managing the authentication and ticket-granting process. By introducing a trusted intermediary between users and services, Kerberos ensures that credentials are never directly exposed to the network, thus reducing the risk of password theft and other forms of credential compromise. The KDC is divided into two critical services: the Authentication Service (AS) and the Ticket Granting Service (TGS).

These two components work together to securely validate user identities and issue tickets that permit access to specific services.

Kerberos operates on the principle of using symmetric key cryptography to secure communications between clients, services, and the KDC. In this model, each principal, whether a user or a service, shares a unique secret key with the KDC. These keys are not transmitted over the network. Instead, the KDC uses them to encrypt tickets and session keys, which are then shared securely with clients and services. Symmetric encryption ensures that only parties possessing the correct key can decrypt and interpret the contents of a message, providing confidentiality and integrity to the authentication process.

The authentication workflow begins when a user, also referred to as a client, requests access to a service within the network. The client first communicates with the Authentication Service component of the KDC to prove its identity. To initiate this process, the client sends an authentication request to the AS, identifying itself with its username or principal name. The AS then verifies the client's identity by locating its corresponding secret key in the KDC's database. If the client's request is valid, the AS issues a Ticket Granting Ticket, or TGT, encrypted using the client's secret key, along with a session key encrypted with the KDC's key.

Upon receiving the TGT, the client must decrypt it using its own secret key, which typically derives from the user's password. This step is crucial because it confirms that only the rightful user, who knows the correct password, can unlock the ticket and obtain the session key. The TGT serves as a reusable proof of identity and can be presented to the Ticket Granting Service to request additional service-specific tickets without re-entering credentials.

When the client needs to access a particular service, it sends a request to the Ticket Granting Service, presenting the TGT and requesting a service ticket for the desired resource. The TGS validates the TGT, ensuring it is still valid and has not expired, and then issues a service ticket. This service ticket contains information about the client, such as its identity and session key, encrypted using the service's secret key known only to the KDC and the service itself. The client also receives a copy of the session key encrypted with its own session key, ensuring secure communication between the client and the service.

The client then contacts the target service, presenting the service ticket and its encrypted session key. The service decrypts the ticket using its own secret key, verifies the client's identity, and establishes a secure communication session using the session key. This mutual authentication process ensures that both the client and the service can trust each other, preventing impersonation and man-in-the-middle attacks.

Another critical principle of Kerberos is its reliance on timestamps and short-lived tickets to limit the risk of replay attacks. Every ticket issued by the KDC includes a validity period, typically lasting several hours, after which the ticket automatically expires. Because Kerberos requires participating systems to maintain synchronized clocks, an attacker cannot reuse a captured ticket outside its validity window. The limited lifespan of tickets reduces the time window in which an attacker could exploit stolen credentials, adding a significant security layer.

Kerberos also emphasizes the concept of realm-based trust models. A realm is a defined administrative boundary within which a single KDC or set of KDCs operate. Each realm manages its own set of principals, policies, and cryptographic keys. In larger networks or in cases where organizations need to collaborate across domains, Kerberos supports cross-realm authentication. This mechanism allows users in one realm to securely access services in another, provided that a trust relationship has been established between the KDCs of the two realms.

One of the most important principles underpinning Kerberos is the idea of minimizing the exposure of reusable credentials. By replacing passwords with temporary tickets and session keys, Kerberos significantly reduces the number of times sensitive information is transmitted over the network. This ticket-based approach not only enhances security but also facilitates Single Sign-On functionality, allowing users to authenticate once and then access multiple services within the same realm without re-authenticating.

While Kerberos was originally designed for academic environments, its architecture and principles have made it highly adaptable to various enterprise ecosystems. Its integration with major operating systems, particularly Microsoft's Active Directory, has cemented its role as a vital component in corporate networks. By following a rigorous, time-tested set of principles, Kerberos provides a secure and efficient method for handling authentication in distributed environments where traditional models fall short. These principles ensure that Kerberos continues to serve as a reliable framework for protecting sensitive assets and facilitating secure communications in complex networks.

# Kerberos Architecture Overview

The Kerberos architecture is designed to address the fundamental problem of secure authentication across an untrusted network. Its architecture follows a client-server model with a centralized component responsible for the distribution of keys and authentication tickets. At the heart of Kerberos is the Key Distribution Center, or KDC, which serves as the trusted intermediary between users and services. Every entity within a Kerberos environment—whether it be a user, a service, or a device—is referred to as a principal and is identified by a unique name within a defined realm. The architecture ensures that principals can securely authenticate with one another without transmitting reusable passwords across the network.

The Key Distribution Center plays the most critical role in the Kerberos ecosystem. It is composed of two essential components: the Authentication Service and the Ticket Granting Service. The Authentication Service is the first point of contact for clients who wish to establish their identity within the network. When a user logs in, the Authentication Service verifies the user's credentials and issues a Ticket Granting Ticket, or TGT. This ticket is encrypted and can only be decrypted by the user's key, which is derived from the user's password. The Ticket Granting Service is responsible for issuing service tickets, which are used to access specific network resources. The KDC maintains a secret key for every principal within its realm, enabling it to securely issue tickets that will later be validated by the intended service.

In addition to the KDC, the Kerberos architecture includes clients and application servers. Clients are typically end-user machines or applications that request access to services. The application servers host the resources or services that users wish to access, such as file servers, databases, or web servers. Each application server must also be registered with the KDC and possess a secret key known only to itself and the KDC. This shared secret is vital for decrypting service tickets and establishing secure sessions with clients.

The architecture is centered around the ticket-based authentication model. Tickets act as temporary credentials that prove a client's identity to a service without requiring the client to repeatedly send its password or other sensitive information. When a user initiates a session, the client system communicates with the Authentication Service to obtain a TGT. This TGT is subsequently used to request service tickets from the Ticket Granting Service. The service ticket allows the client to authenticate to the target application server securely. The use of tickets ensures that sensitive information, such as passwords, are never directly transmitted across the network after the initial login.

The Kerberos architecture also relies heavily on symmetric key cryptography. Each principal shares a secret key with the KDC, and these keys are used to encrypt and decrypt tickets and session keys. When a service ticket is created by the Ticket Granting Service, it is encrypted with the target service's secret key, making it unreadable to anyone except the service itself. Likewise, session keys, which are temporary cryptographic keys used for client-service communication, are encrypted using keys known only to the client and the service. This design ensures confidentiality and integrity of all authentication-related data.

One of the defining features of the Kerberos architecture is its dependency on synchronized time across all entities within a realm. To prevent replay attacks, where an attacker intercepts and reuses valid authentication data, Kerberos enforces strict time-based controls. Each ticket contains timestamps indicating when it was issued and when it will expire. Both clients and servers verify these timestamps before accepting tickets, ensuring that only current and valid tickets can be used for authentication. Typically, Kerberos allows for a slight time discrepancy, but clocks must generally be synchronized within a few minutes to maintain proper ticket validation.

Kerberos operates within a realm, which defines the administrative boundary of its authentication services. A realm is typically aligned with an organization's network or domain. Within a realm, all principals trust the KDC as the sole authority for issuing and validating authentication tickets. In larger or more complex environments, multiple realms may exist. Kerberos supports cross-realm authentication, which allows users from one realm to securely access services in another. This is achieved by establishing trust relationships between the KDCs of the involved realms, creating a chain of trust that enables authentication across distinct administrative domains.

Another important aspect of the Kerberos architecture is its support for mutual authentication. Not only does the client prove its identity to the service, but the service also proves its identity to the client. This two-way authentication ensures that clients are communicating with legitimate services and not malicious imposters. The mutual authentication process is facilitated by the session key provided during the ticket exchange, which is used to encrypt and verify messages between the client and the service.

Kerberos also integrates with other security mechanisms and protocols, making it highly versatile in enterprise environments. For example, in Microsoft Active Directory domains, Kerberos serves as the default authentication protocol, tightly integrated into the broader directory services. Kerberos can also be used in conjunction with services like LDAP for directory lookups or with NFS for secure file sharing in Unix-based systems. The architecture's modular design allows it to function across different platforms and applications, making it a key component in both traditional on-premises networks and modern hybrid environments.

Despite its reliance on centralized components, the Kerberos architecture is designed with scalability in mind. Large enterprises can deploy multiple KDC servers in a master-slave configuration to ensure availability and load balancing. Replicated KDCs can service authentication requests in geographically distributed data centers, maintaining performance and redundancy.

The design of the Kerberos architecture reflects a commitment to securing authentication in open and potentially hostile network environments. By using trusted intermediaries, strong cryptographic practices, and a carefully structured ticketing system, Kerberos achieves a balance between security, efficiency, and flexibility. It is precisely this robust design that has allowed Kerberos to remain a foundational authentication solution in organizations worldwide.

# Key Distribution Center (KDC) Explained

The Key Distribution Center, commonly referred to as the KDC, is the core component of the Kerberos authentication protocol. Without the KDC, the entire Kerberos infrastructure would not function, as it serves as the trusted authority responsible for managing and distributing the cryptographic keys and tickets that secure authentication in the network. The KDC is the heart of the trusted third-party model that Kerberos relies upon, and its role is critical in enforcing secure access to network services while preventing unauthorized access and credential exposure.

The KDC performs two primary functions within a Kerberos environment: it acts as both the Authentication Service (AS) and the Ticket Granting Service (TGS). These two services work in tandem to handle the full authentication lifecycle, from the initial verification of a user's identity to the granting of access to specific network resources. Every client and service within a Kerberos realm depends on the KDC to obtain cryptographic tickets and session keys necessary for secure communication. Because the KDC is trusted by both clients and services, it forms the cornerstone of trust within the realm.

When a user initiates a session by logging into the network, the first interaction occurs with the Authentication Service component of the KDC. The client requests authentication by sending its identity, typically a username or principal name, to the AS. The AS then checks the KDC's database for the corresponding entry, which includes the secret key derived from the user's password. Upon successful verification, the AS issues a Ticket Granting Ticket, or TGT, along with a session key. The TGT is encrypted with the KDC's secret key, while the session key is encrypted using the user's key. This dual-encryption approach ensures that only the rightful user, who possesses the correct password, can decrypt the session key and make use of the TGT.

The Ticket Granting Ticket plays a vital role in the Kerberos protocol, as it allows the user to request service-specific tickets without having to transmit credentials again. Once the user has obtained the TGT, it is sent to the Ticket Granting Service, the second component of the KDC, whenever the user requires access to a specific service within the network. The TGS, upon receiving the TGT, validates it using the KDC's own secret key. If the ticket is valid and has not expired, the TGS issues a service ticket. This ticket is encrypted with the target service's secret key, allowing only the intended service to decrypt and verify the ticket's authenticity.

The KDC's role extends beyond simply issuing tickets. It also serves as the authority for maintaining a centralized database of all principals within its realm. This database includes critical information such as usernames, service names, and the secret keys associated with each principal. Because the KDC holds the master copies of these keys, it is able to generate and encrypt the tickets that clients and services rely on to authenticate securely. This centralized control simplifies key management, as administrators can manage principal information in one location instead of distributing keys manually across multiple systems.

Security within the KDC itself is of paramount importance. Since the KDC holds all secret keys and serves as the single point of trust for authentication within the realm, any compromise of the KDC could potentially jeopardize the entire Kerberos infrastructure. For this reason, KDC servers are often hardened against attacks, placed behind strict firewalls, and configured to limit access only to essential personnel and services. Additional safeguards such as physical security, encryption of stored keys, and regular auditing are commonly employed to protect the integrity and confidentiality of the KDC.

Another critical aspect of the KDC's functionality is its reliance on accurate time synchronization. Kerberos uses timestamps as part of its ticketing system to mitigate replay attacks, ensuring that tickets and authentication data are valid only within a defined time window. To enforce this, both the KDC and all participating clients and services must maintain closely synchronized clocks. The KDC embeds timestamps into the tickets it issues, and clients and services verify these timestamps during the authentication process. If a ticket falls outside the acceptable time skew, typically a few minutes, it is rejected as potentially suspicious or compromised.

The KDC's responsibilities also extend to supporting cross-realm authentication in environments where multiple Kerberos realms are present. In these cases, the KDC establishes trust relationships with KDCs from other realms through shared secret keys or cross-realm tickets. This capability allows users from one realm to access services in another without requiring duplicate credentials or separate authentication mechanisms. The KDC handles the complex task of exchanging and validating inter-realm tickets, ensuring that secure and seamless authentication can occur across organizational or administrative boundaries.

Scalability is another important consideration when designing a KDC infrastructure. In large enterprise environments, relying on a single KDC server would create a potential bottleneck and a single point of failure. To address this, organizations often deploy multiple KDC servers in a master-slave or peer-to-peer configuration. Slave KDCs serve as replicas of the master KDC, handling authentication requests and issuing tickets while periodically synchronizing with the master server to ensure consistency. This distributed approach improves availability, fault tolerance, and performance, particularly in geographically dispersed networks.

The KDC is also deeply integrated into many modern enterprise environments, particularly those that utilize Microsoft Active Directory. In Active Directory domains, the KDC functionality is embedded within domain controllers, which handle both directory services and Kerberos authentication. This integration allows for seamless authentication across Windows-based systems and applications, leveraging the full power of Kerberos while simplifying management through centralized directory services.

In summary, the Key Distribution Center is the foundational component that enables secure authentication and access control within a Kerberos-protected environment. Its ability to manage secret keys, issue tickets, and act as the central point of trust makes it indispensable to the protocol's effectiveness. The KDC not only facilitates secure communication between clients and services but also enforces important security policies such as ticket expiration and mutual authentication. By understanding the role and operations of the KDC, organizations are better positioned to design and maintain resilient authentication infrastructures that protect sensitive systems and data from unauthorized access.

# Authentication Service (AS)

The Authentication Service, commonly abbreviated as AS, is one of the two key components within the Key Distribution Center in a Kerberos environment. Its primary responsibility is to initiate the authentication process by validating the identity of users or clients who wish to access network resources securely. The AS acts as the entry point into the Kerberos authentication workflow, playing a vital role in ensuring that users are who they claim to be before any access tokens or tickets are granted. Without the proper functioning of the Authentication Service, the entire Kerberos ticket-based system would not be able to operate as intended.

When a user first attempts to access the network, the client system interacts directly with the AS. This process starts when the user provides their credentials, typically a username and a password, to their local workstation. The workstation then formulates a request to the Authentication Service, identifying the user's principal name, which uniquely identifies the user within the Kerberos realm. Importantly, at this stage, the user's password is not transmitted across the network. Instead, the system uses the password locally to derive a secret key that will later be used to decrypt the response from the AS.

Upon receiving the request, the Authentication Service queries the KDC's secure database to verify that the principal exists and is valid. This database contains a list of all registered principals within the realm, along with their associated secret keys, which are derived from user passwords or assigned keys for services. If the user's principal is found and active, the AS proceeds to generate a Ticket Granting Ticket, or TGT. The TGT is a critical element in the Kerberos protocol as it allows the user to later request access to specific network services from the Ticket Granting Service, without needing to re-enter their credentials.

The TGT issued by the AS is encrypted with the KDC's secret key, which is only known to the KDC and the Ticket Granting Service. This ensures that only the legitimate KDC infrastructure can later decrypt and validate this ticket when the user presents it to the TGS. In addition to the TGT, the AS generates a session key, which will be used for secure communication between the client and the TGS during subsequent ticket requests. To ensure that this session key is securely delivered to the client, it is encrypted using the client's own secret key derived from the password. This encryption guarantees that only the rightful user, who knows the correct password, can successfully decrypt the session key and proceed further in the authentication process.

The response sent back to the client from the AS consists of two primary elements: the encrypted TGT and the encrypted session key. Once the client receives this package, it uses the secret key derived from the user's password to decrypt the session key locally. This process is significant because it proves that the client possesses the correct credentials without the password ever having been exposed to the network. The decrypted session key is then stored temporarily on the client system, where it will be used to securely request service tickets from the Ticket Granting Service.

The Ticket Granting Ticket also includes a timestamp and a validity period, typically several hours. This built-in expiration ensures that tickets cannot be reused indefinitely, limiting the time window in which a stolen ticket might be exploited. The use of timestamps helps to prevent replay attacks, where an attacker might try to capture and reuse authentication data to impersonate a legitimate user. In addition to timestamps, Kerberos requires all devices participating in the authentication process to maintain synchronized clocks, ensuring the validity of these time-based controls.

The Authentication Service plays a pivotal role in enforcing the initial step of mutual trust within the Kerberos protocol. By securely issuing the TGT and session key, the AS lays the groundwork for secure interactions between the client and the network's services. Since only the KDC can decrypt the TGT later in the process, and only the legitimate client can decrypt the session key, the AS establishes a secure chain of trust that the Ticket Granting Service and application servers will later rely upon.

It is worth noting that the AS does not directly grant access to application services, such as file servers or databases. Instead, its function is limited to confirming the user's identity and granting the TGT, which serves as a reusable credential within the Kerberos realm. Once the client holds a valid TGT, the process of requesting access to specific resources is delegated to the Ticket Granting Service. This separation of duties within the KDC enhances security by compartmentalizing responsibilities and reducing the risk associated with any single component being compromised.

The robustness of the Authentication Service is critical to the security of the overall Kerberos infrastructure. Any weaknesses in the AS could be exploited by attackers seeking unauthorized access to the realm. For this reason, the AS is often deployed in highly secure environments with rigorous controls. This includes measures such as limiting network exposure, implementing strict firewall rules, applying patches promptly, and employing encryption for all communications with the AS.

The AS also plays a vital role in supporting Single Sign-On (SSO) capabilities. By authenticating the user once and issuing a TGT valid for a specified duration, the Authentication Service enables users to access multiple services within the Kerberos realm without needing to re-authenticate. This streamlined approach enhances both security and usability, reducing the number of times credentials are entered and minimizing the likelihood of credential theft through phishing or other attacks.

In modern enterprise environments, the functionality provided by the Authentication Service is seamlessly integrated into directory services like Microsoft Active Directory. In such implementations, the domain controller serves as the KDC, housing both the AS and the TGS. This integration simplifies user authentication processes across Windows domains and other enterprise services that rely on Kerberos for secure access control.

The Authentication Service is a vital guardian of the initial trust relationship in the Kerberos protocol. By issuing secure and encrypted TGTs, verifying user credentials without transmitting passwords, and facilitating ticket-based authentication, the AS plays a foundational role in protecting sensitive enterprise networks from unauthorized access. Its design ensures that authentication is efficient, secure, and scalable, providing the essential first step in establishing trust between users and the resources they wish to access.

# Ticket Granting Service (TGS)

The Ticket Granting Service, or TGS, is a crucial component of the Key Distribution Center within the Kerberos authentication protocol. It operates in conjunction with the Authentication Service to manage secure and efficient access to network resources in a distributed environment. While the Authentication Service is responsible for verifying a user's identity and issuing an initial Ticket Granting Ticket, the TGS takes over the subsequent role of issuing service-specific tickets that allow clients to access particular applications or services without the need to re-enter their credentials. The TGS is the mechanism that facilitates Single Sign-On within the Kerberos protocol, making it possible for users to authenticate once and then access multiple systems within the same realm securely.

Once a user has successfully obtained a Ticket Granting Ticket from the Authentication Service, that user does not directly request access to application servers. Instead, the user's client communicates with the TGS, presenting the TGT as proof of its previously authenticated identity. The Ticket Granting Service then verifies the validity of the TGT, ensuring that it was properly issued by the KDC and that it has not expired or been tampered with. The TGS is able to perform this verification because the TGT is encrypted using the KDC's secret key, which is shared internally between the AS and the TGS. No other entity outside the KDC has the ability to decrypt and validate the TGT, preserving the confidentiality and integrity of the ticket.

After validating the TGT, the TGS moves to the next step of its process: issuing a service ticket that will be used by the client to authenticate to a specific service within the network. The service ticket contains critical authentication information about the client, such as the client's identity, the requested service, a timestamp, a ticket lifetime, and a newly generated session key. This session key is to be used exclusively between the client and the service it is trying to access, establishing a secure communication channel for their interactions.

To ensure that only the intended service can read and validate the service ticket, the TGS encrypts it using the target service's secret key, which is known only to the service itself and the KDC. This encryption guarantees that the service ticket, even if intercepted on the network, cannot be decrypted by unauthorized entities. In parallel, the TGS also provides the client with a copy of the same session key, encrypted using the session key from the TGT exchange. This allows the client to securely communicate with the service by using the shared session key, which remains unknown to potential attackers.

The service ticket issued by the TGS, along with the encrypted session key, is then returned to the client. The client subsequently presents the service ticket to the intended application server, demonstrating its right to access the service without exposing its password or any reusable credentials. The application server decrypts the service ticket using its own secret key and retrieves the session key from within the ticket. This enables the server to initiate mutual authentication and establish an encrypted session with the client.

The Ticket Granting Service enforces strict controls on the validity and usage of service tickets. Each service ticket is issued with a specific validity period defined by the start and expiration times embedded within the ticket. This time-bound mechanism plays an essential role in protecting the Kerberos ecosystem from replay attacks. Even if an attacker were able to capture a valid service ticket, they would only have a limited window of time before the ticket expires and becomes unusable. Additionally, because of the requirement for synchronized clocks between clients, the KDC, and application servers, Kerberos can ensure that tickets falling outside of acceptable time skews are rejected as invalid.

One of the key advantages provided by the TGS is the enablement of Single Sign-On functionality. Since users only authenticate once to obtain a TGT from the Authentication Service, they do not need to re-enter their credentials for every subsequent access to services within the same realm. Instead, the TGT serves as a reusable token that the client can present to the TGS multiple times throughout its validity period. This greatly enhances user experience by eliminating redundant logins, while also improving security by reducing the number of times sensitive credentials are handled and potentially exposed.

The TGS is also instrumental in supporting cross-realm authentication, where users from one Kerberos realm need to access services located in a different realm. In such cases, trust relationships are established between the KDCs of both realms. The TGS can issue a cross-realm ticket that allows a client to interact with the TGS of the target realm. The TGS of the second realm then issues a service ticket for the client, following the same principles and security mechanisms as it would within its own realm. This feature is particularly valuable in large enterprise environments and collaborative networks where resources span multiple domains or organizations.

The Ticket Granting Service must be highly secure and reliable, as it plays a central role in authorizing client access to services across the entire Kerberos-protected network. To this end, the TGS is typically deployed with the same high level of security precautions as the Authentication Service. The TGS runs on the KDC server or servers, which are hardened against attacks, isolated within secure network segments, and subject to rigorous monitoring and access controls. Any disruption or compromise of the TGS can severely impact the availability and security of the Kerberos authentication process, making its protection a top priority for system administrators.

The design of the Ticket Granting Service reflects Kerberos' commitment to security, efficiency, and scalability. By offloading the service ticket issuance from the initial authentication process handled by the AS, the TGS enables Kerberos to manage large volumes of authentication requests without overwhelming a single component. This separation of duties helps reduce latency, distribute workload effectively, and allows organizations to scale their authentication infrastructure to meet the demands of complex and geographically distributed environments.

The Ticket Granting Service is the linchpin in the second phase of the Kerberos authentication process, bridging the gap between the initial identity verification and the granting of specific resource access. Its function is critical in maintaining the security posture of the entire Kerberos protocol, ensuring that only authenticated clients can obtain the necessary tickets to access sensitive services securely and efficiently across the network.

# Kerberos Tickets and Their Lifecycle

In the Kerberos authentication protocol, tickets are fundamental to securing and managing user and service authentication across distributed network environments. A Kerberos ticket is essentially a time-sensitive, encrypted data structure that serves as proof of identity for clients and services within a Kerberos realm. By using tickets, Kerberos eliminates the need for users to repeatedly transmit sensitive credentials such as passwords over the network. The ticketing system not only enhances security but also simplifies access to multiple services through a Single Sign-On experience. Understanding the types of tickets and the stages they pass through is crucial to grasping how Kerberos achieves its security objectives.

Kerberos tickets come in two primary forms: the Ticket Granting Ticket, or TGT, and the service ticket, sometimes referred to as the access ticket. Each of these tickets serves a specific purpose within the Kerberos ticket lifecycle, and both are issued and managed by the Key Distribution Center. The Ticket Granting Ticket is issued by the Authentication Service as the result of a successful login. When a user first authenticates to the Kerberos system by providing a username and password, the client system contacts the Authentication Service. Upon validating the credentials, the AS issues a TGT, which is encrypted using the KDC's secret key and contains important data such as the user's identity, a timestamp, an expiration time, and a session key. The TGT allows the client to request additional service tickets from the Ticket Granting Service without having to repeat the password-based authentication process.

Once the TGT has been issued and securely delivered to the client, it becomes the client's reusable token within the Kerberos realm. For as long as the TGT remains valid, the client can use it to request service tickets for any Kerberos-enabled resource within the realm. When the client needs access to a specific service, such as a file server, database, or web application, it presents the TGT to the Ticket Granting Service along with the name of the desired service. The TGS, after validating the TGT and ensuring it is still within its validity period, issues a service ticket tailored to the requested service.

The service ticket contains information similar to that of the TGT but is specific to the relationship between the client and the target service. It includes the client's identity, the service's identity, a new session key, a timestamp, and an expiration time. The service ticket is encrypted using the secret key of the target service, which ensures that only the intended service can decrypt and validate the ticket. The client also receives a copy of the session key encrypted with its own session key, allowing the client and the service to establish a secure communication channel.

With the service ticket in hand, the client proceeds to contact the target service, presenting the ticket as proof of its identity and authorization. The service decrypts the ticket, validates the client's information, and extracts the session key. This session key is then used to facilitate encrypted communication between the client and the service, completing the mutual authentication process. The service ticket grants the client access for a limited duration, after which a new ticket must be requested from the TGS if continued access is needed.

The lifecycle of Kerberos tickets is governed by strict timing mechanisms that ensure tickets are valid only for a finite period. This design is critical to mitigating risks such as replay attacks, where an attacker could attempt to reuse an intercepted ticket to impersonate a legitimate user. The lifetime of a TGT is typically several hours, while service tickets are often valid for shorter periods depending on the organization's security policies. When a TGT or service ticket expires, the client must obtain a new ticket to continue accessing resources. This time-bound approach ensures that even if a ticket is compromised, the window of opportunity for its misuse is limited.

In addition to expiration times, Kerberos supports ticket renewal. Clients can request a renewal of their TGT before it expires, extending its validity without needing to perform the initial password-based authentication again. This feature enhances usability in long-running sessions or automated processes where constant re-authentication would be impractical. However, renewals are subject to policy-defined limits to prevent indefinite extension of ticket lifetimes.

Another important aspect of the ticket lifecycle is ticket destruction. Once a client no longer needs a TGT or service ticket, or when a session ends, the tickets should be securely discarded to prevent accidental reuse or exposure. In many systems, Kerberos tickets are stored in memory or in protected ticket cache files that are cleared when the user logs out or when the system reboots.

Kerberos tickets also play a role in facilitating delegation. In scenarios where a service needs to act on behalf of a client to access another service, Kerberos supports the concept of ticket forwarding and delegation. The TGS can issue forwardable service tickets, which can then be passed along to downstream services. This allows applications such as web servers or middleware to request additional service tickets on behalf of the original client, enabling complex multi-tier authentication workflows while maintaining security.

Throughout their lifecycle, tickets are carefully protected using strong encryption algorithms. Both the TGT and service tickets rely on symmetric cryptography, using keys that are known only to the KDC, the client, and the target service. This approach ensures that tickets remain confidential and tamper-proof during transmission and storage.

The integrity and security of Kerberos tickets are fundamental to the protocol's effectiveness. The entire system depends on the assumption that tickets cannot be forged, altered, or misused once issued. This is why the protection of the KDC, the secrecy of principal keys, and the correct implementation of ticket expiration and renewal policies are all essential components of a secure Kerberos deployment. A properly managed ticket lifecycle minimizes the risk of unauthorized access and provides organizations with a robust mechanism for enforcing access controls across complex distributed networks.

By leveraging tickets as temporary, encrypted proofs of identity, Kerberos achieves a delicate balance between strong security, efficiency, and user convenience. Tickets not only streamline authentication across multiple services but also ensure that sensitive credentials remain protected at every stage of the authentication process.

# Encryption in Kerberos

Encryption is at the very core of the Kerberos authentication protocol, providing the essential protection that allows secure authentication and communication to occur over potentially hostile and untrusted networks. Without encryption, the entire ticket-based system that Kerberos relies upon would be vulnerable to interception, tampering, and unauthorized access. Kerberos was designed from the outset to protect authentication exchanges using symmetric key cryptography, ensuring that even if an attacker captures data on the network, they would be unable to decipher or manipulate the sensitive information contained in the messages.

Kerberos relies primarily on symmetric key encryption, where the same key is used to both encrypt and decrypt data. Each principal within a Kerberos realm—whether it is a user, a service, or a system—shares a unique symmetric key with the Key Distribution Center. These shared secrets enable the KDC to securely create tickets and session keys that can only be decrypted and verified by their intended recipients. The use of symmetric encryption ensures both confidentiality and integrity for all Kerberos ticket exchanges.

The first critical use of encryption in Kerberos occurs when a client requests a Ticket Granting Ticket from the Authentication Service. After a user inputs their credentials on the client machine, the client's system derives a secret key from the user's password using a cryptographic hash function combined with a salting process to prevent dictionary attacks. This secret key is never transmitted over the network. Instead, it is used locally by the client to decrypt information received from the KDC. When the Authentication Service issues a TGT, it encrypts part of the response, including the session key, using the client's secret key. Only the client who knows the password can decrypt this session key, proving possession of the correct credentials without sending the password across the network.

The Ticket Granting Ticket itself is encrypted with the KDC's master key. This master key is shared only between the KDC's components, specifically the Authentication Service and the Ticket Granting Service. When the client later presents the TGT to the Ticket Granting Service to request access to a specific network resource, the TGS decrypts the TGT using this master key to verify its authenticity and extract the client's identity and session key. The use of encryption here ensures that the TGT cannot be tampered with or reused by an attacker, as only the KDC possesses the necessary key to decrypt and validate the ticket.

When the Ticket Granting Service issues a service ticket, it continues to rely on encryption to protect the ticket from unauthorized access. The service ticket is encrypted using the target service's secret key, which is known only to the service and the KDC. This means that even if the service ticket is intercepted during transmission between the client and the service, it remains unreadable to anyone lacking the appropriate key. The service ticket contains critical information such as the client's identity, a new session key, and a timestamp defining the ticket's validity window. The TGS also provides the client with a copy of the session key, encrypted with the client's session key from the TGT, allowing the client and the service to establish an encrypted communication session.

Kerberos encryption protects not just tickets but also the session-level interactions that follow ticket exchanges. Once the client presents the service ticket to the target service, both the client and the service use the shared session key from the ticket to encrypt and decrypt messages exchanged during their session. This ensures that subsequent data transferred between the client and service remains confidential and cannot be read or altered by an outside party. The session key is temporary and valid only for the duration specified in the ticket's lifetime, further limiting the risk of compromise.

Kerberos has evolved to support a variety of encryption algorithms over time. Originally, Kerberos implementations relied on the Data Encryption Standard (DES), a symmetric encryption standard that has since been deprecated due to its vulnerabilities to brute-force attacks. Modern Kerberos environments now use stronger algorithms such as Advanced Encryption Standard (AES) with key lengths of 128 or 256 bits. AES is widely regarded as a secure and efficient encryption standard, providing robust protection against common cryptographic attacks. Some environments may also use Triple DES (3DES) or RC4, although these algorithms are increasingly being phased out in favor of stronger alternatives like AES.

Encryption also plays a role in protecting the integrity of the data transmitted between Kerberos components. In addition to encrypting tickets and session keys, Kerberos often employs keyed hash functions or Message Authentication Codes (MACs) to ensure that data has not been altered in transit. By combining encryption with integrity checks, Kerberos guarantees that any tampering or corruption of data will be detected by the receiving party.

Time synchronization is closely tied to the use of encryption in Kerberos. Since tickets include timestamps that define their validity period, encrypted tickets must be decrypted and validated against the current system time. This time-sensitive nature of tickets helps mitigate replay attacks, where an attacker attempts to reuse intercepted messages to impersonate a legitimate client. The use of encrypted timestamps ensures that tickets are only valid within a narrow time window, making them useless to attackers who try to exploit old tickets.

Cross-realm authentication, which allows users from one Kerberos realm to access services in another, also relies on encryption to maintain security across administrative boundaries. When two realms establish trust, their KDCs share secret keys that are used to encrypt and decrypt cross-realm tickets. This allows tickets issued in one realm to be recognized and validated in another, facilitating secure authentication across different organizational networks while maintaining the confidentiality of ticket contents.

Kerberos encryption does not operate in isolation but is often paired with additional transport-level security mechanisms. For example, when Kerberos is used in conjunction with other protocols such as LDAP or HTTP, it is common to layer Transport Layer Security (TLS) on top of the session to further protect communications. While Kerberos secures authentication at the application layer, TLS helps protect subsequent data transfers against network-level threats.

The effectiveness of Kerberos relies heavily on the secrecy and proper management of the encryption keys used throughout the system. The KDC must ensure that all stored keys are securely protected and that regular key rotation policies are in place. Similarly, clients and services must take care to protect session keys in memory and during transmission. Encryption in Kerberos is not just about transforming data into an unreadable format; it is about establishing trust between parties, maintaining data confidentiality, preventing unauthorized access, and verifying the integrity of authentication exchanges within the network. The careful and consistent use of encryption throughout the Kerberos protocol is what enables it to serve as a reliable and secure authentication mechanism for enterprise environments.

# Kerberos and Symmetric Key Cryptography

Kerberos is fundamentally built on the principles of symmetric key cryptography, which is the cornerstone of its authentication and ticketing system. Symmetric key cryptography is a type of encryption where the same cryptographic key is used for both encryption and decryption of data. In the context of Kerberos, this model allows users, services, and the Key Distribution Center to establish secure communications and verify each other's identities without exposing sensitive information such as passwords or long-term credentials over the network. The choice of symmetric key cryptography in Kerberos is based on its speed, efficiency, and simplicity when compared to more computationally intensive asymmetric algorithms, which require separate public and private key pairs.

In a Kerberos environment, every principal, whether a client or a service, shares a unique symmetric key with the Key Distribution Center. These keys are essential because they form the basis of trust between the KDC and all entities within the Kerberos realm. The KDC's responsibility is to securely store and manage these keys, which are used to encrypt and decrypt the tickets and session keys that are exchanged during the authentication process. The concept is straightforward: a principal can decrypt only the information that has been encrypted with its unique key, ensuring that no other entity in the network, including potential attackers, can access or alter the encrypted data without possessing the correct key.

The initial use of symmetric key cryptography occurs when a client seeks to authenticate and requests a Ticket Granting Ticket from the Authentication Service. The KDC's database holds a secret key for the client, derived from the client's password. When the Authentication Service generates the TGT, it encrypts the session key portion of the response using this secret key. Only the client, who knows the password and can derive the correct key, can decrypt this response. This mechanism ensures that only the legitimate user can complete the authentication process, since no password is ever transmitted over the network. The TGT itself is also encrypted, but with the KDC's own long-term secret key, which the Ticket Granting Service will later use to validate the ticket and issue service-specific credentials.

The use of symmetric key cryptography continues in the next phase of Kerberos, when the client presents the TGT to the Ticket Granting Service in exchange for a service ticket. The Ticket Granting Service verifies the TGT using the shared KDC key, and upon successful validation, it creates a new service ticket encrypted with the target service's symmetric key. Only the target service, which holds this specific secret key, can decrypt the ticket and verify its contents. Simultaneously, the TGS provides the client with a copy of the session key encrypted using the session key from the TGT. This process enables both the client and the service to establish a mutually trusted and encrypted communication session using the newly shared session key.

The key benefit of symmetric key cryptography in this context is its efficiency. Symmetric algorithms such as Advanced Encryption Standard (AES) allow for fast encryption and decryption of data, which is critical when Kerberos is handling potentially thousands of authentication requests across a large network in real-time. The lightweight nature of symmetric key operations helps ensure that Kerberos can provide robust security without introducing significant performance overhead.

Another critical aspect of symmetric key cryptography in Kerberos is the protection against tampering and unauthorized modifications. Since tickets and session keys are encrypted with keys known only to the intended recipients, any attempt to modify or forge a ticket would be easily detected, as the decryption process would fail or the information inside the ticket would not align with expectations. This provides data integrity alongside confidentiality, which are both essential properties of secure communication in distributed networks.

Kerberos also uses symmetric encryption to protect the session-level exchanges between clients and services. Once the service ticket is successfully presented to the target service and both parties retrieve the session key from the ticket, all subsequent communications can be encrypted using this shared session key. This ensures that any sensitive information exchanged during the session, such as user data or service requests, remains confidential and protected against interception.

Historically, Kerberos started with symmetric encryption algorithms like DES, which provided a baseline level of security at the time of its initial development. However, as cryptographic research advanced and DES was found to be vulnerable to brute-force attacks, Kerberos evolved to support stronger algorithms such as 3DES and, later, AES. Today, AES with 128-bit or 256-bit key lengths is the most commonly used algorithm in modern Kerberos implementations, providing robust protection while adhering to current security standards.

Symmetric key cryptography in Kerberos is not just limited to ticketing and session management but also extends to the concept of cross-realm authentication. In multi-realm environments, where users from one realm need to access services in another, KDCs from different realms establish a shared symmetric key that enables them to exchange cross-realm tickets securely. This inter-KDC trust allows the Kerberos protocol to function seamlessly across administrative boundaries while maintaining the confidentiality and integrity of authentication information.

The reliance on symmetric key cryptography also introduces important operational responsibilities for system administrators. Keys must be securely generated, stored, and rotated periodically to reduce the risk of key compromise. In many enterprise environments, keytab files are used to store service keys securely on servers, allowing them to participate in the Kerberos ticketing process without requiring manual password input. Protecting these keytab files is crucial, as unauthorized access to a service's key would undermine the confidentiality of the encrypted tickets and session keys.

Time synchronization is another factor intertwined with Kerberos' use of symmetric keys. Because tickets are valid only for limited time windows, all systems in the Kerberos realm must have synchronized clocks. This ensures that tickets issued and encrypted by the KDC will be considered valid when decrypted and validated by clients and services using their shared keys. Without tight time synchronization, even correctly encrypted tickets could be rejected as expired or invalid, disrupting the authentication process.

Kerberos demonstrates how symmetric key cryptography can be employed effectively at multiple stages of a secure authentication protocol. By encrypting tickets, session keys, and communications with trusted symmetric keys, Kerberos ensures that identity verification and access control are handled with a high level of security. This approach minimizes the exposure of sensitive credentials, reduces the attack surface within the network, and maintains the performance required to support large-scale enterprise deployments. The durability and efficiency of symmetric key cryptography continue to make it the optimal choice for Kerberos as it operates across both traditional on-premises networks and modern hybrid environments.


# Time Synchronization in Kerberos

Time synchronization is a critical and often overlooked component of the Kerberos authentication protocol. The entire security model of

Kerberos depends heavily on accurate and consistent timekeeping between all entities within a given realm, including clients, servers, and the Key Distribution Center. Without synchronized clocks, the ticket-based system that Kerberos relies on would not function as intended, leaving the network vulnerable to replay attacks, authentication failures, and disruption of services. Kerberos uses time as an additional security control, enforcing the validity of tickets within a predefined time window and limiting their potential misuse.

Kerberos incorporates timestamps into every ticket and authenticator to determine when a ticket was issued and when it will expire. Each Kerberos ticket includes two essential time fields: the start time and the expiration time. When the Key Distribution Center issues a Ticket Granting Ticket or a service ticket, it stamps the ticket with the current time, designating the start of its validity. It then calculates an expiration time based on ticket lifetime policies defined by the administrators. This ensures that tickets cannot be used indefinitely and introduces a self-contained expiration mechanism that limits the window of opportunity in which tickets are valid and effective.

Because of this reliance on accurate timestamps, Kerberos requires that the clocks of all participating systems be synchronized within a narrow tolerance range, often referred to as clock skew. The default allowable clock skew in many Kerberos implementations is typically set to five minutes, although administrators can adjust this threshold depending on organizational policies and infrastructure considerations. If the time on a client, service, or KDC differs from another system by more than the allowed skew, ticket validation will fail. This could result in legitimate authentication requests being denied, causing interruptions in access to critical network services.

The reason Kerberos employs this time-based mechanism is to prevent replay attacks. A replay attack occurs when an attacker captures a valid authentication message, such as a ticket or authenticator, and attempts to reuse it to impersonate a legitimate user. By enforcing strict time constraints, Kerberos ensures that captured tickets cannot be replayed outside of their narrow validity window. Even if an attacker were to intercept a valid ticket or session key, they would only be able to use it within the short period before the ticket expires. After expiration, the ticket is automatically rendered invalid by all participating services and systems.

Authenticators, which are generated by the client and included in the messages sent to services alongside tickets, also play a key role in the time synchronization mechanism. Each authenticator contains a timestamp indicating when it was created. When a service receives a service ticket and an authenticator, it decrypts both, checks the timestamp in the authenticator, and verifies that it falls within the acceptable clock skew window. The service also verifies that the timestamp in the authenticator has not been used previously, ensuring that each authentication attempt is unique and valid only for the current session. This process strengthens the protection against replay attacks by tying each authentication message to a specific moment in time.

Time synchronization is generally achieved through the use of Network Time Protocol, or NTP, which allows devices across a network to synchronize their system clocks to a highly accurate external time source, such as a GPS or atomic clock. Organizations deploying Kerberos typically configure all servers, clients, and KDCs to reference the same NTP servers, creating a unified time base across the entire Kerberos realm. A well-maintained NTP infrastructure helps to ensure that all systems remain within the required time tolerance, reducing the risk of ticket validation failures.

The operational importance of time synchronization in Kerberos extends beyond security concerns to the day-to-day functioning of the protocol. In environments where time drift occurs and devices fall out of sync, users may experience intermittent login issues, failed service ticket requests, and an inability to establish secure sessions with services. Such problems can cause significant disruption, particularly in large enterprise networks where Kerberos serves as the primary authentication mechanism for numerous critical systems and applications.

In addition to using NTP, administrators may implement safeguards such as monitoring tools that alert them to time drift conditions or discrepancies across key infrastructure components. Regular validation of time synchronization status is considered a best practice in Kerberos environments, as even small deviations can lead to a cascade of authentication failures. Furthermore, high-availability Kerberos deployments, where multiple KDCs are distributed across different geographic regions or data centers, place even greater emphasis on time synchronization. Without a consistent time base, cross-realm authentication and inter-KDC trust relationships could become unreliable or insecure.

The security policies governing ticket lifetimes are also directly tied to time synchronization. While shorter ticket lifetimes reduce the risk associated with compromised tickets, they increase the dependency on accurate and timely re-issuance of tickets, making precise timekeeping even more critical. For example, if a ticket's lifetime is limited to just a few hours, but the client's system clock is behind the KDC's clock by more than the allowed skew, the client will be unable to request new service tickets when needed, effectively locking the user out of services until the time discrepancy is corrected.

Kerberos administrators must also consider the impact of daylight saving time adjustments and time zone differences across globally distributed systems. While Kerberos typically relies on Coordinated Universal Time (UTC) to standardize timestamps, improper local time configurations can still introduce inconsistencies if systems fail to correctly handle time offsets or daylight saving transitions. To avoid such pitfalls, administrators should configure all systems in a Kerberos realm to operate using UTC and ensure that NTP configurations account for regional variations in local time.

Another factor closely related to time synchronization in Kerberos is key expiration and rollover. Some Kerberos environments enforce key rotation policies where principal keys are periodically regenerated or replaced. If key updates are time-sensitive and require synchronization across KDCs and services, any discrepancy in system clocks could lead to services being unable to decrypt tickets or session keys, resulting in failed authentications. Ensuring that key rotations and ticket lifetimes are coordinated within a tightly synchronized time framework helps prevent such operational issues.

Time synchronization is not a mere technical requirement in Kerberos but a foundational security control that ensures the protocol can fulfill its intended purpose of securing network authentication. It reinforces the temporary and disposable nature of Kerberos tickets and session keys, prevents the exploitation of expired credentials, and underpins the integrity of mutual authentication between clients, services, and the KDC. The proper implementation and maintenance of time synchronization across a Kerberos realm are critical for sustaining the security, reliability, and efficiency of authentication processes in any enterprise environment.

# Mutual Authentication Mechanism

The mutual authentication mechanism is a critical security feature of the Kerberos protocol, ensuring that both the client and the service verify each other's identities before initiating any secure communication. Unlike unilateral authentication methods, where only the client proves its identity to the server or vice versa, mutual authentication guarantees that both parties can trust that they are interacting with legitimate and authorized entities. In open and potentially hostile network environments, this mechanism is essential for preventing impersonation, man-in-the-middle attacks, and other forms of unauthorized access.

The need for mutual authentication arises from the increasing complexity of distributed systems, where services and clients operate across various domains and platforms. As users access resources in enterprise networks, the security of these interactions cannot rely solely on the client's identity verification. Without mutual authentication, there is a risk that a malicious actor could impersonate a trusted service, tricking users into disclosing sensitive information or submitting confidential data to a compromised endpoint. Kerberos addresses this challenge by embedding a two-way verification process in its ticket-based system.

The process of mutual authentication in Kerberos begins when the client successfully obtains a service ticket from the Ticket Granting Service. The client then initiates communication with the desired service by presenting this service ticket, along with an authenticator. The authenticator is a critical piece of data generated by the client, containing a timestamp and other identifying information, encrypted using the session key shared between the client and the target service. The service ticket itself has already been encrypted by the Ticket Granting Service using the service's long-term secret key, ensuring that only the service can decrypt it.

When the service receives the service ticket and the authenticator, it decrypts the service ticket using its secret key to extract the session key. It then uses this session key to decrypt the authenticator and validate the client's identity. This validation involves checking the client's information and ensuring the timestamp falls within the acceptable time skew, confirming that the request is fresh and has not been replayed by an attacker. At this point, the service has verified the client, but the mutual authentication process requires the client to also verify the service.

To complete mutual authentication, the service responds by sending a message back to the client. This response is typically a copy of the timestamp from the client's authenticator, incremented by one and encrypted using the same session key. When the client receives this response, it decrypts the message using the session key it already possesses and checks the timestamp. The incremented timestamp serves as proof that the service not only decrypted the authenticator but also possesses the session key, which could only be obtained by successfully decrypting the service ticket using the service's own long-term key. This proves to the client that the service is genuine and trustworthy.

The exchange of encrypted timestamps, combined with the protection provided by session keys and service tickets, forms the backbone of mutual authentication in Kerberos. It ensures that both parties confirm their identities before continuing with any data transfer or application-layer interaction. The use of session keys prevents eavesdropping, as all messages between the client and the service following the mutual authentication phase can now be encrypted using this shared secret.

Mutual authentication also plays a crucial role in securing applications against common network threats. One of the most notable risks mitigated by this mechanism is the man-in-the-middle attack. In this type of attack, an adversary positions themselves between the client and the service, attempting to intercept or alter communications. However, because Kerberos requires both client and service to prove possession of specific cryptographic keys through mutual authentication, an attacker who lacks these keys cannot successfully complete the exchange. The inability to produce a valid incremented timestamp, encrypted with the correct session key, will immediately reveal the attacker's presence.

Additionally, mutual authentication enhances user trust and system integrity within enterprise networks. Users can be confident that they are interacting with legitimate services, reducing the risk of data leakage or exposure to rogue servers. This is particularly important in environments where users regularly access sensitive applications, such as financial systems, HR platforms, or proprietary business tools. By preventing service impersonation, Kerberos helps organizations maintain the confidentiality and authenticity of interactions across the network.

Mutual authentication is tightly coupled with other Kerberos security features, such as time synchronization and session key management. Without synchronized clocks across clients, servers, and the KDC, timestamp validation could fail, disrupting the mutual authentication process. Similarly, improper protection or compromise of session keys could undermine the integrity of the exchange, highlighting the importance of secure key management practices in any Kerberos deployment.

In addition to its standard use within the Kerberos protocol, mutual authentication is also leveraged when Kerberos is integrated with other technologies. For instance, when Kerberos is used in conjunction with SSL/TLS or within web-based applications, the underlying mutual authentication framework helps secure additional layers of communication, extending trust beyond just the Kerberos exchange. In Microsoft Active Directory environments, where Kerberos is the default authentication protocol, mutual authentication ensures that users accessing network resources like file shares, print services, and internal web applications can rely on secure, verified sessions.

Mutual authentication also plays a key role in advanced Kerberos features such as delegation. In constrained delegation scenarios, where one service must act on behalf of a user to access another service, the initial mutual authentication provides the assurance that both the user and the intermediary service are valid participants in the chain of trust. This layered verification is essential for maintaining security as tickets and session keys are forwarded or delegated within complex workflows.

The implementation of mutual authentication within Kerberos illustrates the protocol's holistic approach to network security. By requiring both the client and the service to authenticate each other, Kerberos ensures that trust is always verified from both directions, reducing vulnerabilities and reinforcing secure communications in even the most complex and distributed enterprise environments. The simplicity and effectiveness of mutual authentication are among the reasons Kerberos has remained a cornerstone of enterprise network security for decades.

# Kerberos Realms and Cross-Realm Authentication

In the Kerberos authentication protocol, the concept of a realm defines the logical boundary within which all authentication and ticketing operations take place. A realm is essentially an administrative domain or trust boundary where a single Key Distribution Center serves as the trusted third-party authority responsible for issuing and managing authentication tickets. All users, services, and devices registered within a given realm rely on that realm's KDC to securely authenticate and authorize access to network resources. The realm establishes a trust context, ensuring that all entities within the domain can rely on the KDC to validate identities and manage ticket issuance. The design of realms in Kerberos reflects a fundamental principle of security: the segmentation of trust into distinct administrative zones.

Each Kerberos realm is identified by a unique name, typically represented in uppercase letters, such as EXAMPLE.COM or CORP.LOCAL. This naming convention helps distinguish realms from one another, particularly when organizations manage multiple realms or when realms from different organizations need to interact. Inside a realm, all principals—whether they are users, services, or host machines—are registered with the realm's KDC. The KDC manages a centralized database containing each principal's unique secret key, which is essential for generating tickets and establishing secure sessions.

While a single Kerberos realm is sufficient for small to medium-sized environments, larger enterprises or organizations with multiple independent business units often require multiple realms. The use of multiple realms becomes even more common when separate organizations need to collaborate while maintaining control over their respective authentication infrastructures. In such scenarios, Kerberos supports cross-realm authentication, which enables users from one realm to securely access services in another realm without requiring duplicate credentials or parallel authentication systems.

Cross-realm authentication is achieved by establishing trust relationships between the KDCs of different realms. These relationships are typically symmetric, meaning that if Realm A trusts Realm B, then Realm B reciprocates by trusting Realm A. The trust is based on the exchange of shared secret keys between the KDCs. Specifically, the administrators of each realm generate a key for the other realm's KDC, creating what is known as a cross-realm trust. This shared key allows the KDCs to encrypt and decrypt tickets exchanged between realms, enabling seamless authentication for users requesting services outside their home realm.

The process of cross-realm authentication begins when a user from one realm, for example, user@REALM-A.COM, requests access to a service in another realm, such as service@REALM-B.COM. The client system starts by obtaining a Ticket Granting Ticket from the KDC in its home realm, REALM-A.COM. Once it has a valid TGT, the client requests a cross-realm Ticket Granting Ticket for REALM-B.COM from its own KDC. The KDC in REALM-A.COM responds by issuing a special cross-realm TGT, encrypted using the shared secret key established between the two realms' KDCs.

The client then uses this cross-realm TGT to communicate with the KDC in REALM-B.COM. By presenting the cross-realm ticket to the

Ticket Granting Service of REALM-B.COM, the client effectively gains the ability to request service tickets for any resource registered within the second realm. The TGS in REALM-B.COM decrypts the cross-realm TGT using the shared key, verifies the client's identity and the ticket's validity, and then issues a service ticket encrypted with the secret key of the target service. From this point on, the client interacts with the service in REALM-B.COM as though it were a native user of that realm, completing the mutual authentication process and establishing a secure session.

One of the key advantages of this cross-realm model is that it preserves the autonomy of each realm while allowing for controlled interoperability. Each realm retains full control over its principals, policies, and KDC infrastructure, while the trust relationship enables secure and verifiable authentication across realms. This flexibility is particularly useful in federated environments, where different organizations or divisions need to collaborate while maintaining independent administrative control over their respective systems.

In large-scale Kerberos deployments, cross-realm authentication can involve multi-hop trust relationships, where two realms that do not share a direct trust relationship authenticate through one or more intermediary realms. This is known as transitive trust. For example, if REALM-A.COM trusts REALM-B.COM and REALM-B.COM trusts REALM-C.COM, users in REALM-A.COM can access services in REALM-C.COM by traversing the chain of trust through REALM-B.COM. The Kerberos client automatically requests and follows the appropriate sequence of cross-realm tickets to complete the authentication path. While transitive trust provides scalability for complex environments, it also introduces additional administrative overhead and security considerations, as each realm in the chain must be secured and properly managed.

Cross-realm authentication introduces challenges that administrators must address to maintain a secure and reliable environment. One such challenge is key management. The secret keys used to establish cross-realm trust relationships must be securely generated, distributed, and rotated according to best practices. Weaknesses or compromises in these keys could undermine the security of cross-realm authentication. Additionally, administrators must ensure that ticket lifetimes, policies, and clock synchronization are consistent across realms to avoid ticket validation errors or unintended access issues.

Authorization policies also play a significant role in cross-realm scenarios. While Kerberos handles authentication, authorization decisions are typically left to the target service. A service in REALM-B.COM may need to apply additional access control checks to determine whether a user from REALM-A.COM is permitted to access the requested resource. This layered approach to authentication and authorization helps organizations enforce local security policies while still allowing external users to authenticate successfully.

Kerberos realms and cross-realm authentication reflect the protocol's emphasis on flexibility and scalability in securing network resources. By segmenting trust into manageable domains and providing mechanisms to bridge those domains securely, Kerberos supports a wide range of organizational structures, from small businesses with a single realm to multinational enterprises with complex, interconnected trust relationships. The design of realms and cross-realm authentication ensures that Kerberos can adapt to the evolving needs of distributed systems while maintaining the confidentiality, integrity, and availability of authentication processes across diverse environments.

# Kerberos and Single Sign-On (SSO)

Kerberos is widely recognized as one of the foundational technologies enabling Single Sign-On, or SSO, across enterprise networks. Single Sign-On is the ability for users to authenticate once and subsequently gain access to multiple independent systems, applications, or services without being prompted to log in again during the same session. This capability greatly enhances the user experience by reducing repetitive authentication steps, while simultaneously increasing security by minimizing the exposure of user credentials across various touchpoints in the network. The ticket-based architecture of Kerberos is specifically designed to deliver this functionality, making it a key enabler of SSO within many large-scale IT environments.

At the core of the Kerberos-based Single Sign-On process is the concept of issuing reusable tickets. When a user initially logs in to their workstation or system within a Kerberos realm, their client interacts with the Authentication Service of the Key Distribution Center to validate their credentials. Upon successful authentication, the client receives a Ticket Granting Ticket, or TGT, which is encrypted and bound to the user's identity and a session key. The TGT serves as a reusable token that allows the client to request service-specific tickets from the Ticket Granting Service without re-authenticating with the user's password.

With this TGT in hand, the client can silently interact with the Ticket Granting Service whenever the user attempts to access a Kerberos-protected service within the network. Instead of asking the user to re-enter their username and password, the client automatically presents the TGT to the TGS. The Ticket Granting Service, after validating the TGT, issues a service ticket for the requested resource, which is then presented to the target service. This entire sequence occurs transparently to the user, who perceives the experience as seamless access to multiple systems after a single login.

The strength of Kerberos-based SSO lies in its ability to eliminate the need for repeated authentication while maintaining strong security controls. Once the initial authentication has been performed and the TGT issued, there is no need for the user's password to traverse the network again. The reuse of the TGT and service tickets, each of which is encrypted and time-limited, ensures that authentication is both secure and efficient. This model reduces the risk of credential theft, as sensitive information is exposed only once during the login process and is subsequently replaced by temporary cryptographic tickets.

Kerberos SSO is particularly well-suited for environments where users need to access a variety of services distributed across different servers and applications. In an enterprise setting, an employee might need access to file servers, email systems, intranet portals, collaboration tools, and databases throughout the day. Without SSO, this would typically require repeated login prompts and password submissions, leading to inefficiencies and user frustration. Kerberos eliminates this friction by granting access to all authorized services within the realm, provided that valid tickets are available.

From an operational perspective, Kerberos SSO simplifies user authentication while simultaneously reducing the administrative burden on IT teams. When users no longer need to manage multiple passwords for different systems, there are fewer help desk requests for password resets, fewer cases of forgotten credentials, and a lower chance that users will adopt insecure password practices such as writing down passwords or reusing weak credentials across different services. By relying on a single point of authentication through the KDC, organizations also gain centralized control over authentication policies, improving security governance.

The secure ticketing mechanism used in Kerberos ensures that Single Sign-On does not compromise security. Each service ticket issued by the TGS is time-bound, meaning it has a clear expiration window after which it becomes invalid. This expiration policy mitigates risks associated with ticket theft or misuse. Even if an attacker were to capture a valid service ticket, it would only remain useful for a limited period. Additionally, tickets are cryptographically protected using symmetric encryption, meaning they cannot be easily forged or altered.

Mutual authentication, another inherent feature of Kerberos, further strengthens the SSO model. Not only does the user authenticate to services using valid tickets, but the services also prove their identity back to the client. This mutual verification process ensures that clients do not inadvertently communicate with rogue or impersonated services. Combined with the encryption of session-level communications using shared session keys, mutual authentication safeguards data exchanges within an SSO session against interception and man-in-the-middle attacks.

Kerberos-based SSO integrates seamlessly with modern enterprise directory services, most notably Microsoft Active Directory. In Active Directory environments, Kerberos is the default authentication protocol used for SSO across the domain. When a user logs into a Windows domain-joined workstation, Kerberos automatically authenticates the user to the Active Directory domain and enables SSO for all domain-registered services, including file shares, printers, internal websites, and other network applications. This integration is one of the primary reasons why Kerberos has remained a dominant force in enterprise authentication strategies.

Kerberos SSO can also extend into hybrid and cross-platform environments. Many organizations leverage Kerberos-based SSO in Unix/Linux networks, web applications, and cloud services through mechanisms such as Kerberos-enabled LDAP services or HTTP Negotiate authentication. Additionally, with the help of federated identity protocols like SAML and OAuth, organizations can integrate Kerberos SSO with external systems or cloud-based services, creating a seamless authentication experience that crosses on-premises and cloud boundaries.

One of the challenges associated with Kerberos-based SSO is managing the ticket lifecycle efficiently. Since tickets are valid only for specific durations, organizations must strike a balance between security and usability. Short ticket lifetimes increase security by reducing the window of ticket exposure but may require users to re-authenticate or renew tickets more frequently. Conversely, longer ticket lifetimes improve user convenience but may introduce additional risks if tickets are compromised. Administrators configure ticket lifetimes, renewability policies, and session timeout parameters to align with organizational security requirements and user experience expectations.

The effectiveness of Kerberos SSO also depends on maintaining synchronized system clocks across all clients, services, and KDCs. Since ticket validity relies on timestamp verification, even minor discrepancies in system time can disrupt the seamless nature of SSO, leading to authentication failures and the need for manual re-authentication. Ensuring accurate time synchronization via protocols like NTP is an essential component of any Kerberos-based SSO deployment.

Kerberos Single Sign-On embodies the core philosophy of reducing repetitive authentication steps while ensuring that security remains uncompromised. Its ticket-based system, rooted in symmetric key cryptography and mutual trust, creates a secure framework for user authentication across complex, distributed environments. This balance of usability and security has made Kerberos one of the most enduring and widely adopted solutions for delivering SSO capabilities in modern enterprise networks. By enabling users to focus on their tasks without repeated interruptions for authentication, while still providing robust protection against unauthorized access, Kerberos continues to play a pivotal role in enhancing both productivity and cybersecurity in organizations worldwide.

# Kerberos and Active Directory

Kerberos and Microsoft Active Directory are deeply intertwined, forming the backbone of secure authentication in Windows-based enterprise networks. When Microsoft introduced Windows 2000, it incorporated Kerberos as the default authentication protocol within Active Directory domains, marking a significant shift away from the older NTLM protocol. Since then, Kerberos has remained a foundational element of Active Directory's security model, providing a robust, scalable, and efficient method of authenticating users, services, and computers across enterprise networks.

Active Directory is Microsoft's centralized directory service that stores information about users, computers, and resources within a domain. It facilitates identity management, access control, and policy enforcement across an organization's IT infrastructure. At its core, Active Directory relies on the Kerberos protocol to perform secure authentication for users and services attempting to access resources within the domain. Every domain controller in an Active Directory environment acts as a Kerberos Key Distribution Center, performing both the Authentication Service and Ticket Granting Service functions. This integration ensures that all entities within the domain can leverage Kerberos' ticket-based system to authenticate securely without constantly transmitting passwords across the network.

When a user logs into a workstation that is a member of an Active Directory domain, the system automatically initiates a Kerberos authentication request to a domain controller. The user's credentials, typically in the form of a username and password, are used to derive a secret key locally on the client machine. This key is then used to decrypt the session key and Ticket Granting Ticket received from the domain controller's Authentication Service. The TGT allows the client to request service tickets from the Ticket Granting Service component of the domain controller, granting access to various network services such as file shares, email systems, print servers, and web applications registered within the domain.

The Kerberos implementation in Active Directory includes several enhancements specific to Windows environments. One such enhancement is the integration of Group Policy, which allows administrators to define password policies, account lockout thresholds, ticket lifetimes, and other security settings directly through Active Directory. These policies are enforced during the Kerberos ticketing process, ensuring that authentication adheres to the organization's specific security requirements.

Service Principal Names, or SPNs, are another critical component of Kerberos within Active Directory. SPNs are unique identifiers assigned to services running on servers in the domain. They allow the Kerberos Ticket Granting Service to locate and issue service tickets for specific services when a client requests access. Administrators must correctly configure SPNs for services such as SQL Server instances, IIS web applications, and custom enterprise applications to ensure that Kerberos authentication functions properly. Misconfigured SPNs can lead to authentication failures or fallback to less secure protocols like NTLM.

Active Directory also facilitates Kerberos delegation, a feature that allows a service to act on behalf of a user when accessing downstream services. Delegation is commonly used in scenarios such as web applications accessing backend databases on behalf of users. Kerberos supports two forms of delegation within Active Directory: unconstrained delegation and constrained delegation. Unconstrained delegation allows a service to access any resource in the domain using the client's delegated credentials, while constrained delegation restricts access to only specified services. Microsoft later introduced resource-based constrained delegation, which enables service owners to control delegation permissions directly on the target resource, providing more granular control over delegated access.

The Kerberos integration with Active Directory also supports mutual authentication, which ensures that both the client and the service confirm each other's identities before establishing a secure session. When a user requests access to a service, the service ticket issued by the TGS includes information encrypted with the service's secret key. The service decrypts the ticket, retrieves the client's identity, and returns a response encrypted with the shared session key, proving its authenticity to the client. This exchange prevents impersonation and man-in-the-middle attacks by confirming that both parties are legitimate participants in the session.

Kerberos within Active Directory plays a vital role in enabling Single Sign-On capabilities. Users who log into their domain-joined Windows workstations automatically receive a TGT, which they can reuse to access multiple services throughout the domain without re-entering credentials. This seamless experience enhances user productivity while minimizing the risks associated with password fatigue and repeated credential submission.

In addition to supporting traditional Windows-based services, Kerberos within Active Directory is frequently leveraged to secure access to web applications and cloud-based resources. Many organizations use Kerberos to authenticate users to intranet applications through protocols such as HTTP Negotiate or Integrated Windows Authentication, allowing browsers like Microsoft Edge, Google Chrome, or Mozilla Firefox to transparently use the user's Kerberos tickets to access web resources within the domain.

Kerberos is also used in hybrid cloud scenarios, where organizations integrate on-premises Active Directory with cloud identity services such as Azure Active Directory. While Azure Active Directory primarily relies on modern authentication protocols like OAuth and OpenID Connect, organizations can establish trust between on-premises Active Directory and cloud-based resources using federation services, allowing users to authenticate once in their Kerberos-secured on-premises environment and gain access to cloud applications through Single Sign-On.

Administrators managing Kerberos in Active Directory environments must ensure that the domain controllers and all member systems are time-synchronized to prevent ticket validation failures. Since Kerberos relies on strict time-based controls to prevent replay attacks and to enforce ticket expiration, Active Directory domains typically use the

Windows Time Service (W32Time) combined with Network Time Protocol to maintain accurate time synchronization across all systems.

Security considerations are central to the operation of Kerberos in Active Directory. Because domain controllers act as KDCs and store all principal keys within the Active Directory database, they are high-value targets for attackers. Protecting domain controllers involves implementing multiple layers of security, including restricting administrative access, segmenting domain controllers into secure network zones, and regularly auditing Kerberos-related logs and events to detect suspicious activity such as ticket forgery attempts or brute-force attacks against service principal accounts.

Kerberos is also instrumental in supporting security-enhanced authentication mechanisms within Active Directory, such as smart card logon. In smart card authentication, the user's credentials are protected by a physical card containing a cryptographic chip, and Kerberos is used to issue tickets after verifying the smart card credentials. This strengthens user authentication by incorporating two-factor verification, where possession of the smart card and knowledge of the corresponding PIN are both required.

The partnership between Kerberos and Active Directory is a powerful one, delivering a highly scalable, secure, and efficient authentication system that forms the foundation for most Windows enterprise networks today. By tightly integrating Kerberos with Active Directory's management, policy enforcement, and directory services, Microsoft has created an authentication ecosystem capable of serving organizations of all sizes, from small businesses to multinational corporations. This integration continues to evolve, adapting to modern security requirements and supporting both on-premises and cloud-based infrastructures across the modern IT landscape.

# Kerberos Version 4 vs. Version 5

Kerberos has undergone significant evolution since its inception, with Version 4 and Version 5 marking two distinct stages in the development of the protocol. Both versions share the same foundational goal: to provide secure authentication over untrusted networks using a trusted third-party model and symmetric key cryptography. However, Version 5 of Kerberos was designed to address critical limitations and shortcomings found in Version 4, incorporating new features, enhanced security, and broader interoperability that made it more suitable for enterprise environments and heterogeneous systems.

Kerberos Version 4 was developed at the Massachusetts Institute of Technology (MIT) in the 1980s as part of Project Athena. It introduced the core concepts of the protocol, including the use of a centralized Key Distribution Center, the ticket-based authentication mechanism, and the reliance on symmetric key cryptography to secure communications between clients and services. Version 4 was revolutionary for its time, offering a viable solution to the problem of securing authentication across open networks. It defined the use of Ticket Granting Tickets and service tickets, along with the notion of authenticators to prevent replay attacks.

Despite its innovations, Version 4 of Kerberos suffered from several limitations. One of the most significant issues was its lack of support for modern encryption algorithms. Version 4 relied heavily on the Data Encryption Standard, or DES, which by the 1990s was increasingly seen as insufficiently secure due to its short key length and vulnerability to brute-force attacks. Additionally, Version 4 lacked support for internationalization, as it did not properly handle non-ASCII character sets, limiting its usability in multinational organizations where principal names and passwords may include characters outside the English alphabet.

Another drawback of Kerberos Version 4 was its limited ticket lifetime and renewal capabilities. Tickets issued in Version 4 had a fixed lifetime, and there was no standardized mechanism for renewing them, which posed challenges in environments where long-running processes required continued access to services without frequent re-authentication. Moreover, Version 4 did not natively support cross-realm authentication, making it difficult to establish trust relationships between distinct Kerberos realms without implementing non-standardized workarounds.

Recognizing these and other limitations, the Internet Engineering Task Force (IETF) introduced Kerberos Version 5 in 1993 through RFC 1510, which was later updated by RFC 4120. Kerberos Version 5 retained the core principles of Version 4 but implemented significant improvements to enhance security, flexibility, and compatibility with modern networked environments. One of the most notable enhancements in Version 5 was the introduction of a modular framework that allowed for the use of stronger encryption algorithms. In contrast to Version 4's reliance on DES, Version 5 supports multiple encryption types, including Triple DES (3DES), Advanced Encryption Standard (AES), and others, allowing administrators to select algorithms based on their security needs and compliance requirements.

Kerberos Version 5 also resolved the issue of cross-realm authentication by introducing a standardized mechanism for establishing trust between realms. This improvement enables users from one Kerberos realm to securely access services in another realm without the need for duplicate accounts or manual key exchanges. The cross-realm authentication model in Version 5 is scalable and flexible, supporting both direct and transitive trust relationships between realms. This capability has made Version 5 particularly valuable in large enterprise environments and federated networks where collaboration across administrative boundaries is essential.

Another key enhancement in Version 5 is its support for ticket renewal and postdating. In Version 5, tickets can be issued with a renewable flag, allowing clients to request an extension of the ticket's validity period without requiring the user to re-authenticate. This feature is particularly useful in environments where automated processes, such as background services or batch jobs, require long-term access to resources. Additionally, Version 5 introduced the concept of postdated tickets, which can be issued with a start time in the future, providing greater control over when access to services becomes valid.

Kerberos Version 5 also improved on the network protocol aspects of the system. It introduced better support for UDP and TCP transport mechanisms, which helped alleviate issues related to packet fragmentation in large ticket exchanges. While Version 4 operated primarily over UDP, which could struggle with large packets due to size limitations, Version 5 allowed clients and KDCs to switch to TCP when necessary, providing more reliable communication in networks with restrictive or fragmented conditions.

A significant difference between Version 4 and Version 5 lies in the handling of authorization data. In Version 4, tickets did not include structured fields for passing detailed authorization information, limiting the protocol's ability to convey granular access control data. Version 5 addressed this limitation by supporting authorization data fields within tickets, allowing additional information—such as access control lists, user roles, or group memberships—to be securely transmitted alongside authentication data. This enhancement has made Kerberos Version 5 a better fit for environments that require fine-grained access control beyond basic authentication.

Version 5 also introduced internationalization support, addressing the global nature of modern IT environments. It allows for principal names, realm names, and passwords to be expressed in a broader set of character encodings, including Unicode. This has enabled Kerberos to be used in multinational organizations where users and services may require non-ASCII characters for proper identification.

Another improvement is related to password management. While Version 4 did not include native mechanisms for password changing, Version 5 provides a standardized password change protocol, enabling users to securely update their passwords within the Kerberos environment. This functionality simplifies administration and improves compliance with security policies that mandate regular password rotation.

Kerberos Version 5 also adopted a more modular and extensible design, paving the way for integration with other security protocols and services. For example, it is commonly used with LDAP-based directory services and has become a key component of Microsoft's Active Directory infrastructure. The improvements introduced in Version 5 have enabled Kerberos to serve as a core authentication system not only for Unix and Linux environments but also for Windows domains and hybrid cloud infrastructures.

Despite their shared roots, Kerberos Version 4 and Version 5 represent two distinctly different stages in the evolution of the protocol. While Version 4 laid the groundwork for secure ticket-based authentication in distributed systems, Version 5 expanded the protocol's capabilities, enhanced its security, and positioned it as the de facto standard for enterprise authentication across diverse platforms and industries. Today, Version 5 is the actively supported and widely deployed version of Kerberos, with Version 4 largely considered obsolete and phased out of most modern implementations due to its security weaknesses and lack of flexibility.

# Setting Up a Kerberos Environment

Setting up a Kerberos environment is a critical process that requires careful planning and precise configuration to ensure secure and efficient authentication across a network. Kerberos operates on the principle of a centralized Key Distribution Center that manages the issuance and validation of tickets for clients and services. Implementing Kerberos involves several key steps, including the installation and configuration of the KDC, the creation of realms, the registration of principals, and the integration of Kerberos clients and services into the overall infrastructure. Each stage is essential to establish a functioning authentication system that leverages the strengths of Kerberos to secure access to network resources.

The first step in setting up a Kerberos environment is to design the realm structure. A realm represents the logical and administrative boundary within which Kerberos operates. The realm name is typically derived from the organization's domain name, expressed in uppercase letters. For example, an organization with the domain example.com may create a Kerberos realm called EXAMPLE.COM. This realm will define the trust zone for all principals, including users and services, that rely on the KDC for authentication. In larger organizations, multiple realms may be necessary to separate administrative domains or to support cross-realm authentication.

Once the realm has been defined, the next step is to deploy the Key Distribution Center. The KDC serves as the backbone of the Kerberos environment and must be installed on a secure, dedicated server. The KDC consists of two main components: the Authentication Service and the Ticket Granting Service. These services are responsible for issuing the Ticket Granting Ticket after initial client authentication and for issuing service tickets when clients request access to specific services. The KDC must be installed using a trusted Kerberos distribution, such as MIT Kerberos or Heimdal Kerberos, depending on the organization's platform requirements.

During the installation of the KDC, administrators will configure the KDC database, which stores information about all registered principals and their associated secret keys. This database is the most sensitive part of the Kerberos infrastructure, as it contains the cryptographic secrets that protect the realm. Therefore, it is essential to secure the KDC server through hardened configurations, including restricting physical and remote access, applying regular security patches, and isolating the server in a protected network segment.

Once the KDC is operational, the next phase is to create the principals that will participate in the Kerberos environment. A principal is any entity—such as a user, service, or host—that will request or accept Kerberos tickets. Principals follow a naming convention such as user@REALM for user accounts or service/hostname@REALM for services. The KDC administrator uses Kerberos utilities like kadmin to create principals and assign initial passwords or keytab files. Keytabs are files that securely store encrypted keys for services, allowing them to authenticate with the KDC automatically without requiring manual password entry.

An important consideration during this phase is to register all services that will participate in Kerberos authentication. For example, if file servers, databases, or web applications need to accept Kerberos tickets, each of these services must have a corresponding principal in the KDC database. Additionally, service principal names must be unique and correctly associated with the appropriate hostnames to ensure that clients can locate and authenticate to services correctly. Failure to configure service principals properly can result in authentication failures or fallback to weaker protocols.

With the KDC and principals configured, the next step is to set up Kerberos clients. Clients can include user workstations, servers, or any system that needs to request tickets from the KDC. On Unix and Linux systems, clients are configured using the krb5.conf file, where administrators specify the default realm, the addresses of the KDC servers, and any additional Kerberos-related settings such as ticket lifetimes or preferred encryption types. On Windows systems within an Active Directory domain, Kerberos is configured automatically, as Active Directory domain controllers serve as KDCs for the domain.

After the clients are configured, they can begin to authenticate with the KDC. When a user logs into their system, the client software automatically requests a Ticket Granting Ticket from the Authentication Service using the user's credentials. The TGT is then cached locally and reused to request service tickets from the Ticket Granting Service when accessing domain services. This process enables Single Sign-On functionality, reducing the need for users to repeatedly enter passwords as they navigate between different services within the realm.

A key aspect of setting up a Kerberos environment is time synchronization. Kerberos relies on synchronized system clocks across the KDC, clients, and services to prevent replay attacks and to enforce ticket validity periods. Administrators must ensure that all systems within the Kerberos realm use a reliable time source, typically provided by Network Time Protocol servers. Without proper time synchronization, clients may experience ticket validation errors, leading to disruptions in service availability.

Testing and validation are crucial before rolling out Kerberos in production. Administrators should verify that clients can successfully obtain TGTs, request service tickets, and authenticate to services without errors. Tools such as kinit, klist, and kvno can be used to troubleshoot ticket requests, ticket caches, and service ticket acquisition on Unix-based systems. On Windows systems, tools like klist and event logs provide insights into Kerberos authentication flows and potential misconfigurations.

Security hardening should be applied to every component in the Kerberos environment. This includes configuring secure encryption types such as AES, enforcing strong password policies for user principals, regularly rotating keys and keytab files, and auditing Kerberos logs for suspicious activity. Access to the KDC should be limited to trusted administrators, and backups of the KDC database should be encrypted and stored securely to protect against data loss or compromise.

Setting up a Kerberos environment is a multi-step process that combines infrastructure planning, secure system configuration, and ongoing management. By carefully designing the realm structure, securing the KDC, registering principals, configuring clients, and enforcing time synchronization and security policies, organizations can establish a strong foundation for secure authentication across their network. A properly implemented Kerberos environment enhances both the security and efficiency of authentication processes, reducing the attack surface and supporting scalable access control in complex enterprise networks.

# Configuring the KDC Server

Configuring the Key Distribution Center server is one of the most critical stages in deploying a secure and functional Kerberos authentication infrastructure. The KDC acts as the trusted third party in the Kerberos environment, issuing and managing authentication tickets for all users and services within the realm. Its correct configuration determines the overall security, stability, and efficiency of the authentication process across the entire network. The KDC houses both the Authentication Service and the Ticket Granting Service, and its database contains all principal accounts, encryption keys, and policy information. Due to its vital role, setting up the KDC requires meticulous attention to detail and adherence to best practices.

The process begins with selecting the appropriate Kerberos implementation, typically MIT Kerberos or Heimdal Kerberos, both of which are widely used in Unix and Linux environments. In Windows-based environments, Microsoft's implementation of Kerberos is integrated into Active Directory, and domain controllers serve as the KDCs. For Unix or Linux-based Kerberos realms, the administrator installs the KDC server package provided by the distribution's package manager or compiles it from source. Once installed, the KDC must be configured using specific configuration files, the most critical of which is the kdc.conf file.

The kdc.conf file defines the parameters of the KDC, including the default realm, logging settings, ticket lifetimes, and supported encryption types. The default realm specified in this configuration must match the organizational naming convention, such as EXAMPLE.COM, and will govern all principals managed by the KDC. In addition to realm settings, the administrator must configure access control policies, including restrictions on which clients and services can request tickets, as well as the paths to the KDC database and other critical components.

Next, the Kerberos realm must be initialized by creating the KDC's principal database. This database is a secure repository that stores every principal's cryptographic key and metadata. The initialization process typically involves running a command-line utility, such as kdb5_util for MIT Kerberos, to create and format the database. During this step, the administrator is prompted to define the master key for the KDC. The master key is used to encrypt the database itself and must be safeguarded carefully, as its compromise would endanger the entire Kerberos infrastructure.

Once the database has been initialized, the administrator can begin creating principals. Principals include user accounts, service accounts, and host principals, each following a standard naming format such as user@REALM, service/hostname@REALM, or host/hostname@REALM. User principals represent individual users who will authenticate to the realm, while service and host principals represent services or systems that will accept Kerberos tickets. Using administrative tools like kadmin or kadmin.local, administrators can add principals to the database, assign secure initial passwords, and configure policies for each account, such as minimum password lengths and expiration dates.

Another key aspect of KDC configuration is the generation and distribution of keytab files for service principals. A keytab is a file containing the service's encrypted key and is used to allow services to authenticate with the KDC without manual password input. After creating service principals in the KDC database, administrators use utilities like ktadd to generate keytab files and securely transfer them to the servers hosting the services. Keytab files must be protected with strong file permissions, as unauthorized access to a keytab could allow an attacker to impersonate the service.

Ticket lifetime policies also play a crucial role in KDC configuration. In the kdc.conf file, administrators define default and maximum ticket lifetimes, renewal periods, and other time-based settings that dictate how long tickets remain valid. Shorter ticket lifetimes enhance security by reducing the window of opportunity for ticket misuse, but they may increase the frequency of ticket renewals. Conversely, longer lifetimes improve convenience but may introduce additional risk if a ticket is compromised. Striking the right balance based on the organization's security posture is essential.

Encryption types supported by the KDC must also be configured based on security requirements. Modern Kerberos environments typically favor AES encryption with 128-bit or 256-bit keys, but compatibility with older systems may necessitate enabling additional algorithms such as RC4 or 3DES. However, weak encryption types like DES should be avoided entirely, as they are no longer considered secure. The kdc.conf file allows administrators to specify preferred encryption types and disable deprecated algorithms to enforce strong cryptographic standards across the realm.

Logging and auditing are vital components of KDC server configuration. The kdc.conf file includes logging directives that define where Kerberos logs should be written and which events should be recorded. Logs capture important information such as successful and failed authentication attempts, ticket requests, and administrative actions performed on the KDC database. Regularly reviewing these logs is critical for detecting suspicious activity, troubleshooting authentication failures, and maintaining compliance with security policies.

Once the KDC configuration is complete, administrators start the KDC service and verify that it is listening on the appropriate network ports, typically UDP and TCP ports 88. The KDC must be reachable by all clients and services within the realm, and network firewall rules should be configured to allow traffic to and from the KDC on the required ports while blocking unnecessary or untrusted connections.

Additionally, time synchronization is a mandatory aspect of KDC server setup. The KDC, along with all clients and services, must synchronize their system clocks to prevent issues related to ticket expiration and replay protection. Configuring Network Time Protocol on the KDC and all participating systems ensures that timestamps included in Kerberos tickets are accurate and within the acceptable time skew window, usually five minutes by default.

Finally, redundancy and high availability are critical considerations for the KDC. In production environments, it is common to deploy multiple KDC servers, with one serving as the master and others as slaves. The master KDC handles principal administration and database updates, while slave KDCs replicate the master database and provide backup authentication services in case the master becomes unavailable. This distributed model ensures that Kerberos authentication remains available even in the event of server failures or network outages.

Configuring the KDC server is a complex and sensitive task that establishes the foundation for the entire Kerberos environment. A properly configured KDC enforces security policies, issues secure tickets, manages principal accounts, and provides the trust anchor for all authentication operations within the realm. By carefully tuning settings, protecting sensitive files and keys, and implementing robust operational practices, administrators ensure that the KDC functions securely and reliably as the core of the Kerberos infrastructure.


# Configuring Kerberos Clients

Configuring Kerberos clients is an essential step in enabling secure authentication within a Kerberos realm. While the Key Distribution Center serves as the centralized authority for issuing tickets and managing principals, clients are the entities that interact with the KDC to request and use those tickets. Clients can include user workstations, application servers, or any system that needs to authenticate to services within the Kerberos realm. Proper client configuration ensures that authentication requests are directed to the correct KDC, tickets are correctly issued and stored, and services can securely interact with users and applications across the network.

The configuration process begins by installing the necessary Kerberos client software on the system. Most Unix and Linux distributions come with Kerberos client packages that include essential tools such as kinit, klist, kvno, and the Kerberos libraries required for ticket management and secure communication. On these systems, the krb5.conf file serves as the primary configuration file, where administrators define key parameters to enable proper communication between the client and the KDC. This configuration file is typically located in the /etc directory and must be consistent across all clients to ensure a smooth authentication process.

One of the first settings to define in the krb5.conf file is the default realm. This realm should match the Kerberos realm configured on the KDC, typically written in uppercase, such as EXAMPLE.COM. The default realm parameter ensures that when a client requests a ticket and does not explicitly specify a realm, it will default to the organization's primary Kerberos realm. In multi-realm environments, the krb5.conf file can also include mappings that associate specific domain names with their corresponding realms, allowing clients to automatically select the correct realm based on the target hostname.

Next, the client configuration must specify the location of the KDCs and administrative servers for the realm. Under the realms section of the krb5.conf file, administrators define one or more KDC servers that the client can contact when requesting tickets. This can include both a master KDC and any replica KDCs deployed for high availability. The configuration should also specify the hostname of the Kerberos administration server, which is used by administrative tools like kadmin to perform principal management tasks. It is common practice to include both IP addresses and fully qualified domain names to ensure proper resolution and redundancy in case of network issues.

The krb5.conf file also defines domain-to-realm mappings, typically found under the [domain_realm] section. These mappings help clients determine which realm to use when attempting to authenticate to services within specific domains. For example, a mapping of .example.com = EXAMPLE.COM ensures that any hostname within the example.com domain will default to the EXAMPLE.COM realm when performing Kerberos authentication.

Once the krb5.conf file is properly configured, the client system is ready to participate in the Kerberos authentication workflow. The typical authentication process begins when a user logs into the system or explicitly requests a Ticket Granting Ticket by using the kinit command. The kinit utility prompts the user for their password and contacts the KDC's Authentication Service to obtain a TGT. Upon successful authentication, the TGT and session key are stored in a local credential cache, allowing the user to request service tickets from the KDC's Ticket Granting Service without re-entering their credentials.

The client's ticket cache is a temporary storage area where TGTs and service tickets are held. On Unix and Linux systems, this cache is often stored as a file in the /tmp directory or maintained in memory, depending on the configuration. Administrators can use the klist utility to inspect the contents of the cache, viewing details such as ticket lifetimes, renewability, and associated realms. If a ticket expires or is no longer needed, users can destroy it using the kdestroy command, which clears the ticket cache and requires the user to re-authenticate.

In addition to user authentication, clients often need to be configured to support Kerberos-enabled services. For example, if a server hosts a Kerberized service such as an NFS share, web application, or database, it must have a service principal registered in the KDC and a corresponding keytab file installed locally. The keytab file contains the encrypted key associated with the service principal, allowing the service to authenticate to the KDC automatically. Administrators must place this file in a secure directory with restrictive file permissions to prevent unauthorized access.

For applications running on the client to leverage Kerberos, they must be compiled with or linked to Kerberos libraries and configured to use Kerberos as the authentication mechanism. This can include settings in application-specific configuration files, environment variables, or command-line options. For example, SSH can be configured to use

Kerberos for authentication by setting the appropriate options in the ssh_config and sshd_config files, such as enabling GSSAPIAuthentication and configuring KerberosTicketCleanup. Similarly, web browsers like Firefox or Chrome can be configured to use Kerberos Single Sign-On by enabling integrated authentication for trusted domains.

Time synchronization is another critical factor in client configuration. Kerberos relies on time-sensitive tickets, and if a client's system clock is out of sync with the KDC, ticket requests will be rejected due to invalid timestamps. All clients must use Network Time Protocol or another reliable time synchronization mechanism to ensure that their clocks remain within the acceptable clock skew window, typically five minutes. Failure to maintain synchronized clocks across clients and KDCs is one of the most common causes of Kerberos authentication failures.

Security hardening should also be considered during client configuration. This includes enforcing strong local password policies, protecting credential caches by limiting file permissions, and restricting access to Kerberos utilities to authorized users. Administrators may also configure the client to prefer stronger encryption types, such as AES, by specifying the desired ciphers in the krb5.conf file.

Finally, administrators must test the Kerberos client configuration to ensure that it is functioning correctly. This involves verifying that the client can obtain a TGT using kinit, that tickets are properly cached and renewed, and that the client can successfully access Kerberized services within the realm. Troubleshooting tools like klist and verbose logging options within applications can assist in identifying and resolving issues.

Configuring Kerberos clients correctly is a foundational step for achieving secure and seamless authentication across the network. By establishing proper realm mappings, defining KDC locations, securing ticket caches, and integrating Kerberos with applications and services, administrators ensure that clients can fully leverage the security and efficiency benefits that Kerberos provides. A well-configured client infrastructure supports not only strong authentication but also the broader goals of Single Sign-On and centralized identity management across enterprise environments.

# Managing Kerberos Principals

Managing Kerberos principals is one of the core administrative responsibilities in maintaining a secure and functional Kerberos environment. Principals are the unique identities recognized by the Kerberos Key Distribution Center, representing users, services, and host machines within a realm. Every authentication operation within Kerberos depends on the proper creation, configuration, and management of these principals. Without an organized approach to principal management, the realm can become disorganized, less secure, and more difficult to troubleshoot or scale. A principal in Kerberos follows a naming format that typically includes a primary identifier, an instance, and a realm. For example, a user principal might look like alice@EXAMPLE.COM, while a service principal might take the form of nfs/server01.example.com@EXAMPLE.COM.

The process of managing principals usually begins by creating user principals. User principals represent individual accounts for human users who will authenticate to the Kerberos realm and request tickets to access network services. Using administrative tools such as kadmin or kadmin.local, administrators can create new user principals by specifying their names and assigning initial passwords. It is important to follow consistent naming conventions when managing user principals to ensure that they are easily recognizable and align with the organization's broader identity management policies. In most cases, the user principal will match the user's organizational username, such as jdoe@EXAMPLE.COM. Once created, the user principal is stored in the KDC's principal database along with its associated encryption keys and metadata.

Service principals are another critical category of Kerberos principals. These identities represent services or applications within the network that accept Kerberos tickets from clients. Examples include services like HTTP for web applications, NFS for file servers, and host principals for secure shell logins to specific machines. Service principals follow a format that includes the service type and the fully qualified domain name of the host, such as HTTP/webserver.example.com@EXAMPLE.COM. Each service principal must have a corresponding keytab file generated by the KDC administrator. This file contains the encrypted key that allows the service to authenticate with the KDC and validate client tickets without requiring manual password input. Protecting keytab files is a critical security task, as unauthorized access to them could result in ticket forgery or impersonation attacks.

Host principals represent machines within the Kerberos realm and are used primarily by system services such as SSH or system daemons that require Kerberos authentication. These principals follow the naming convention host/hostname@REALM and are essential for secure communication between client systems and servers. Host principals are often created during the initial system enrollment process when machines are added to the Kerberos realm, particularly in environments where Kerberos is integrated with configuration management or provisioning tools.

An important aspect of managing Kerberos principals is applying and enforcing principal policies. Policies govern security settings for principals, such as minimum password length, password complexity requirements, password expiration intervals, and account lockout thresholds. By defining policies within the KDC and applying them to user and service principals, administrators ensure that the organization's security standards are enforced consistently. For example, a policy might require that all user passwords be at least 12 characters long, include both uppercase and lowercase letters, and expire every 90 days. Policies can also define password reuse restrictions to prevent users from cycling through a small set of passwords during resets.

Principals can also be configured with additional flags that dictate specific behaviors. These flags may include disallowing password changes, requiring pre-authentication, or marking an account as a service principal. Pre-authentication is particularly important for user principals, as it prevents attackers from requesting encrypted tickets that could be used for offline brute-force attacks against weak passwords. By requiring pre-authentication, the KDC ensures that the client must first present a timestamp encrypted with the user's key, verifying possession of the correct password before receiving a TGT.

Periodically auditing and cleaning up principals is an important administrative task to maintain the health and security of the Kerberos environment. Over time, principals may become outdated, particularly in large organizations where users change roles, leave the organization, or where services are decommissioned. Stale user and service principals represent potential security risks if left unmanaged. Attackers could attempt to exploit unused accounts to gain unauthorized access. Regularly reviewing the list of active principals, disabling unused accounts, and removing obsolete service principals helps reduce the attack surface and ensures that only necessary identities remain active in the KDC database.

Another key area of principal management is key rotation. To reduce the risk of key compromise, administrators should periodically rotate the encryption keys associated with both user and service principals. For service principals, this process involves generating a new key and updating the corresponding keytab files on the service hosts. For user principals, key rotation typically occurs when users change their passwords. Automating key rotation and enforcing periodic password changes through principal policies further strengthens the realm's security.

In environments where Kerberos integrates with other directory services, such as LDAP or Microsoft Active Directory, principal management may extend to synchronizing identity information between systems. For example, when Kerberos is used alongside Active Directory, user accounts in the directory automatically map to Kerberos principals within the domain. This integration simplifies identity management by enabling administrators to manage principal attributes, such as group memberships and access controls, from a centralized directory service.

Administrators must also manage cross-realm principals when configuring trust relationships between Kerberos realms. Cross-realm principals are special accounts created to facilitate authentication between two realms. These principals typically follow a naming convention such as krbtgt/REALM-B@REALM-A, where REALM-A and REALM-B represent the names of two separate Kerberos realms. The cross-realm principals enable the secure exchange of tickets and session keys between realms, supporting users who need to access resources outside of their home realm.

Monitoring and logging principal activity is essential for maintaining the security and operational integrity of the Kerberos realm. The KDC generates logs that capture information about principal usage, including ticket requests, authentication failures, and administrative actions such as principal creation or deletion. Regular review of these logs helps detect anomalies, such as repeated failed login attempts or unusual ticket requests that could indicate unauthorized access attempts or misconfigurations.

Ultimately, the management of Kerberos principals forms the operational core of the Kerberos infrastructure. Effective principal management ensures that the authentication system is secure, organized, and adaptable to the organization's evolving needs. From creating new user accounts to configuring service principals, applying security policies, rotating keys, and auditing account usage, administrators must take a proactive and disciplined approach to managing principals. The health of the Kerberos realm, its ability to enforce secure authentication, and its resistance to attacks depend on diligent and ongoing principal management practices.

# Kerberos Keytab Files

Kerberos keytab files are a critical component in automating the authentication process for services within a Kerberos-secured environment. A keytab file contains one or more pairs of Kerberos principals and their associated encryption keys. These keys are used by services to authenticate to the Kerberos Key Distribution Center without requiring manual password entry or interactive user intervention. In essence, a keytab file allows a service to prove its identity to the KDC by using the stored cryptographic secrets securely and automatically. This automation is essential for non-interactive services such as web servers, file servers, databases, or background processes that need to participate in Kerberos authentication workflows.

The creation of a keytab file begins when an administrator generates a service principal within the KDC database. For example, if a network file server needs to support Kerberos authentication, the administrator would create a service principal such as nfs/server01.example.com@EXAMPLE.COM. Once the service principal is registered, the administrator uses Kerberos administrative tools, such as kadmin or kadmin.local, to extract the principal's keys into a keytab file. This is typically done using the ktadd command, which generates the keytab and writes the encrypted key for the specified principal to the file. The resulting keytab file is then securely transferred to the service host, where it will be used to authenticate with the KDC when service tickets are requested by clients.

The structure of a keytab file consists of one or more records, each containing the principal name, the encryption type, the version number of the key, and the encrypted key itself. Multiple keys may be included in a single keytab file to accommodate scenarios where services operate under more than one principal or where multiple encryption types are used to ensure compatibility across different client configurations. Keytab files are binary files and are not intended to be edited manually. Instead, administrators manage them using dedicated Kerberos utilities such as ktutil or through scripted automation processes.

One of the most important aspects of managing keytab files is ensuring their security. Because a keytab file contains the cryptographic equivalent of a service's password, unauthorized access to a keytab file could allow an attacker to impersonate the service or decrypt sensitive authentication exchanges. For this reason, keytab files must be protected using strict file system permissions, typically allowing access only to the service account under which the application or daemon runs. For example, an HTTP service using a keytab to authenticate to the KDC should store the file in a secure directory readable only by the web server's user account.

Keytab files play a crucial role in enabling Kerberos-enabled services to authenticate users securely. When a client requests access to a service, it presents a service ticket obtained from the KDC. The service, in turn, uses the keytab file to decrypt the ticket using the appropriate key. This process validates the ticket's authenticity, confirms the client's identity, and allows the service to extract the session key necessary for securing subsequent communications. Without the keytab file, services would be unable to decrypt incoming tickets or establish trust with the client, breaking the Kerberos authentication workflow.

An additional benefit of keytab files is their role in supporting automated processes. In environments where scheduled tasks, background jobs, or system-level daemons need to perform Kerberos-authenticated actions, keytab files enable these processes to authenticate silently in the background. For example, a backup system that uses Kerberos to securely access network shares can reference a keytab file in its job scripts to obtain the necessary service tickets without human intervention. This automation simplifies system operations while ensuring that security remains consistent with Kerberos' ticket-based model.

Administrators must periodically rotate the keys contained in keytab files to minimize the risk of key compromise and to comply with organizational security policies. Key rotation involves generating a new encryption key for the service principal and updating both the keytab file and the KDC database with the new key. The ktadd command, combined with the -k option, is typically used to generate a fresh keytab file reflecting the updated key. After updating the keytab, the service must be restarted or signaled to reload its configuration to ensure that it uses the new key during subsequent Kerberos exchanges.

Another consideration in managing keytab files is ensuring that they support the necessary encryption types for compatibility with client systems. Modern Kerberos environments prioritize strong encryption types, such as AES-256, but may require additional encryption algorithms, such as AES-128 or RC4, to accommodate older clients or legacy applications. When generating keytab files, administrators can specify the preferred encryption types to be included, helping to balance security and interoperability within the network.

In complex environments, services may operate under multiple Kerberos principals to support different hostnames, interfaces, or functions. In such cases, administrators can store multiple principal entries in a single keytab file, or they can generate and manage separate keytab files for each principal as needed. The decision to consolidate or separate keytab files depends on organizational policies, service architecture, and security considerations.

The distribution and storage of keytab files should be tightly controlled. Keytab files should be transferred securely using encrypted channels such as SCP or SFTP and should never be exposed to unsecured network transfers or stored in shared directories accessible to unauthorized users. In environments with centralized configuration management, administrators often leverage tools such as Ansible, Puppet, or Chef to automate the secure deployment and update of keytab files across the infrastructure.

Administrators should also take care when backing up keytab files. While it is important to include keytabs in system backups to facilitate recovery, these backups must be encrypted and access-controlled to prevent key disclosure. In the event of a suspected compromise of a keytab file, the affected service principal's keys should be rotated immediately, and the compromised keytab should be removed and replaced with a new, securely generated version.

Kerberos keytab files are indispensable for maintaining the operational security and automation capabilities of Kerberos-enabled services. By securely managing and rotating keytab files, administrators ensure that services can seamlessly authenticate to the KDC, validate client tickets, and participate fully in the Kerberos trust model. The proper handling and protection of keytab files is not only a technical requirement but also a key element of maintaining the overall security posture of a Kerberos-based authentication infrastructure.

# Kerberos Authentication Workflow

The Kerberos authentication workflow is a structured sequence of interactions designed to securely validate the identities of users and services within a network. It is based on the principle of using encrypted tickets and session keys to establish mutual trust between clients, services, and the Key Distribution Center. The workflow is divided into distinct stages, each with a specific function aimed at preventing unauthorized access, eliminating password exposure over the network, and facilitating secure, time-limited access to resources. The ticket-based design of Kerberos ensures that sensitive credentials, such as user passwords, are used sparingly and replaced by cryptographically protected tickets for subsequent authentication steps.

The workflow begins when a user logs into a client machine that is configured as part of the Kerberos realm. The user supplies their credentials, typically a username and password. These credentials are used locally by the client to derive a symmetric key that corresponds to the user's principal key stored on the Key Distribution Center. The client then initiates communication with the Authentication Service component of the KDC, sending an Authentication Service Request that includes the user's principal name and a request for a Ticket Granting Ticket. At this point, no password is transmitted over the network, maintaining the confidentiality of the user's credentials.

Upon receiving the request, the Authentication Service searches its database for the user's principal and retrieves the corresponding secret key. If the principal is valid and active, the Authentication Service generates a Ticket Granting Ticket and a session key. The TGT is encrypted with the KDC's master key, ensuring that only the KDC's Ticket Granting Service can decrypt and validate it later. The session key, on the other hand, is encrypted using the user's secret key, which was derived from the password provided during login. This dual encryption ensures that only the rightful user can decrypt the session key while preserving the security of the TGT.

The client receives the encrypted TGT and session key from the Authentication Service. Using the key derived from the user's password, the client decrypts the session key and stores both the TGT and session key in the local ticket cache. From this point onward, the user no longer needs to provide a password for accessing services within the realm, as the TGT serves as proof of initial authentication and can be reused to request additional service tickets.

When the user attempts to access a Kerberos-protected service, such as a file server, database, or web application, the client contacts the Ticket Granting Service to request a service ticket. The client sends a Ticket Granting Service Request, which includes the previously obtained TGT and an authenticator. The authenticator is a time-stamped message encrypted with the session key received from the Authentication Service. This authenticator demonstrates that the client possesses the valid session key and that the request is recent, helping to prevent replay attacks.

The Ticket Granting Service decrypts the TGT using the KDC's master key and validates its contents, ensuring the ticket has not expired and that the authenticator's timestamp falls within the acceptable clock skew window. If the request is valid, the TGS generates a service ticket specifically for the target service. This service ticket contains the client's identity, a new session key, and ticket lifetime data. It is encrypted using the target service's secret key, which only the service and the KDC know. Additionally, the TGS sends the client a copy of the session key encrypted with the client's session key from the TGT.

The client receives the service ticket and the encrypted session key, stores them in the ticket cache, and proceeds to contact the target service directly. To establish a secure connection, the client sends a Service Request message to the service, presenting the service ticket and a new authenticator encrypted with the freshly provided session key. The service decrypts the ticket using its secret key, extracts the session key, and decrypts the authenticator to verify the client's identity and the freshness of the request.

At this stage, mutual authentication takes place. The service generates a response containing the timestamp from the client's authenticator, incremented by one, and encrypts this response using the session key shared with the client. When the client receives this response, it decrypts it using the same session key and verifies that the timestamp has been correctly incremented. This step proves that the service is genuine and that it possesses the correct key to decrypt the service ticket, completing the mutual authentication process and establishing a trusted session.

Once mutual authentication is confirmed, the client and service can securely exchange information using the session key to encrypt and decrypt their communications. This session key protects the confidentiality and integrity of data shared between the client and the service, preventing eavesdropping or tampering by unauthorized parties. The session key remains valid for the lifetime specified in the service ticket, after which a new ticket must be requested to continue secure interactions.

Throughout the Kerberos authentication workflow, tickets are designed to be time-limited. Both the TGT and service tickets include timestamps that define their valid usage windows, reducing the risk of ticket reuse by attackers. If a ticket expires, the client must either renew the TGT if it is still within the renewable window or re-authenticate with the Authentication Service by providing the user's credentials again.

The ticketing mechanism at the heart of the Kerberos workflow minimizes the need to transmit sensitive credentials across the network. After the initial login, users authenticate to services using tickets and session keys without exposing their password again. This greatly reduces the attack surface for password interception and strengthens the network's overall security posture. The combination of centralized ticket management by the KDC, mutual authentication, and session key-based encryption makes the Kerberos authentication workflow both secure and efficient, supporting large-scale deployments across complex, distributed environments.

# Delegation in Kerberos

Delegation in Kerberos is a powerful feature that allows a service to act on behalf of a user when accessing other services within the same Kerberos realm or across trusted realms. This capability is essential in modern distributed applications where intermediary services often need to access additional backend systems to fulfill client requests. Delegation ensures that this process can be carried out securely while preserving the user's identity throughout the transaction chain. Without delegation, a service would not have the authority to request resources from other services on behalf of the user, severely limiting the flexibility of complex multi-tier architectures.

The need for delegation arises frequently in enterprise environments. A common scenario involves a user accessing a web application, and that application needing to query a database or a file server on the user's behalf. In a non-delegated model, the web application could only access these backend services using its own service principal, thereby losing the context of the original user. Delegation solves this problem by enabling the intermediary service to forward or obtain Kerberos tickets that represent the user, allowing the service to perform actions while preserving the user's security identity.

Kerberos supports several types of delegation, each with varying levels of security and control. The simplest form is known as unconstrained delegation. With unconstrained delegation, a service is granted the ability to use the user's Ticket Granting Ticket to request service tickets to any other resource within the Kerberos realm. This model is highly flexible but introduces security risks if not carefully controlled, as the delegated service could misuse the user's TGT to impersonate the user for any service within the realm. In this model, when a client presents a service ticket to the delegated service, the ticket includes the user's TGT. The service then uses this TGT to obtain additional service tickets from the Ticket Granting Service for any backend system it needs to access.

While unconstrained delegation offers broad capabilities, it is generally recommended only for highly trusted services due to the elevated security risks. For this reason, Kerberos introduced constrained delegation, which limits the backend services that a delegated service can access on behalf of a user. With constrained delegation, the delegated service is only permitted to obtain service tickets for specific services that have been pre-approved by an administrator. This restriction significantly reduces the risk of misuse, as the intermediary service cannot impersonate the user to unauthorized or unrelated systems.

Configuring constrained delegation involves defining trust relationships between the intermediary service and the specific backend services it is allowed to access. In Microsoft Active Directory environments, for example, administrators can configure constrained delegation settings using the delegation tab in the service account's properties within Active Directory Users and Computers. Administrators specify exactly which service principal names the intermediary service is allowed to request tickets for, enforcing a more secure and predictable delegation model.

Kerberos also supports a further refinement of constrained delegation called resource-based constrained delegation. Unlike traditional constrained delegation, where permissions are defined on the intermediary service account, resource-based constrained delegation defines permissions on the target service account itself. This reversal of control allows the owners of the backend services to define which services are allowed to delegate access, providing more granular and decentralized control over delegation relationships. Resource-based constrained delegation is particularly useful in environments with complex access control policies or in multi-domain setups where central control is less practical.

In all delegation models, the security of the user's credentials and tickets remains a top priority. Kerberos uses encrypted tickets and session keys to ensure that only authorized services can decrypt and use delegated credentials. For example, when a client authenticates to a service that supports delegation, the client's ticket includes a forwardable flag. This flag indicates that the client allows its credentials to be forwarded to other services. Without this flag, the service would be unable to use the user's ticket to obtain additional service tickets, effectively preventing delegation.

Forwardable tickets play a key role in enabling delegation. When the intermediary service presents the client's forwardable ticket to the Ticket Granting Service, the TGS verifies that the ticket is valid and then issues a new service ticket for the backend resource. This ticket appears as though it were issued directly to the client, allowing the intermediary service to access the resource as if it were the user. The backend service, upon receiving this ticket, assumes it is communicating directly with the user and applies access controls and audit logging accordingly.

Delegation also integrates seamlessly with mutual authentication, another foundational principle of Kerberos. When an intermediary service accesses a backend service on behalf of the user, both parties still perform mutual authentication using the issued service tickets and session keys. This ensures that neither the intermediary nor the backend service can be impersonated or spoofed by malicious actors within the network.

One of the challenges with delegation is balancing flexibility with security. While delegation simplifies the architecture of many enterprise applications, it also increases the potential attack surface if services are improperly trusted. Administrators must carefully evaluate which services truly require delegation and ensure that delegation is granted only where absolutely necessary. In addition, regular audits should be conducted to review delegation permissions and validate that they remain aligned with the organization's security policies.

Delegation is frequently used in Single Sign-On workflows, particularly in web-based applications. In such scenarios, a user might authenticate to a front-end web server using Kerberos and then require that the web server access a back-end SQL Server database using the user's credentials. Delegation allows this interaction to happen without prompting the user for additional credentials, preserving a seamless user experience while maintaining secure authentication across each layer of the application.

Kerberos delegation also plays a vital role in supporting complex cloud and hybrid architectures. In cloud environments, organizations often integrate on-premises Kerberos authentication with cloud services that need to access internal resources on behalf of users. Delegation enables these scenarios by allowing trusted services to securely bridge authentication between different environments while preserving the user's identity across both on-premises and cloud workloads.

Through its delegation mechanisms, Kerberos provides organizations with the flexibility to build scalable and secure applications that require multi-tier authentication workflows. Whether using unconstrained delegation for trusted services or constrained delegation for tightly controlled access scenarios, Kerberos ensures that identity propagation occurs securely and efficiently across distributed systems. The ability to securely delegate user identities to intermediary services is one of the reasons Kerberos continues to be a cornerstone in enterprise authentication and access control frameworks.

# Kerberos Constrained Delegation

Kerberos constrained delegation is an advanced security feature designed to limit the scope of delegation in multi-tiered authentication environments. Unlike unconstrained delegation, where a service can impersonate a user to access any service within a Kerberos realm, constrained delegation restricts which specific services the delegated service can access on behalf of a user. This limitation addresses some of the security risks associated with the broad permissions of unconstrained delegation, giving administrators greater control and visibility over which services are authorized to act on a user's behalf within the network. Constrained delegation is especially important in environments with strict access control policies or where regulatory compliance requires tighter management of user identities and credentials.

The fundamental purpose of constrained delegation is to provide a secure method for intermediary services to request service tickets on behalf of users, but only to a defined list of target services. This model is commonly used in enterprise scenarios where a front-end application, such as a web server, needs to interact with a backend database or file server, but where administrators want to ensure that the web server cannot use delegated credentials to access other unrelated systems. By enforcing a service-specific delegation policy, constrained delegation minimizes the risk of credential misuse if the intermediary service is compromised.

Constrained delegation is configured at the level of the service principal in the Key Distribution Center database, but in practice, it is often managed through a directory service such as Microsoft Active Directory. Within Active Directory, constrained delegation settings can be defined via the properties of the service account, typically using the Delegation tab available in Active Directory Users and Computers or via PowerShell and group policies. When configuring constrained delegation, administrators select the specific service principal names, or SPNs, that the intermediary service is allowed to delegate to. This list forms the delegation policy, and the intermediary service is restricted to requesting service tickets only for the listed services.

The process begins when a user initiates authentication to the intermediary service, such as by accessing a web application. The client's Kerberos ticket, which includes a forwardable flag, allows the intermediary service to use the ticket for delegation. Once the intermediary service has the user's forwardable ticket, it contacts the Ticket Granting Service to request a service ticket to a backend resource on behalf of the user. The TGS, upon receiving the request, checks the constrained delegation policy associated with the intermediary service's principal. If the target service is listed in the policy, the TGS issues the service ticket; if not, the request is denied, enforcing the constraint.

This mechanism preserves the original user's security context throughout the transaction. When the intermediary service presents the service ticket to the backend system, the backend interprets the connection as originating from the user, not the intermediary service itself. This enables the backend service to apply user-specific access controls, audit logs, and authorization policies as if the user had directly accessed the backend resource. This continuity of identity is crucial in scenarios where the backend service must enforce granular permissions based on user roles, group memberships, or security classifications.

One of the security advantages of constrained delegation is that it prevents delegated services from gaining unauthorized access to sensitive resources. In unconstrained delegation, the intermediary service effectively has the user's Ticket Granting Ticket and can use it to request tickets for any service in the Kerberos realm. This creates a significant security concern if the intermediary service is compromised, as an attacker could leverage the unrestricted TGT to impersonate the user across the entire network. Constrained delegation mitigates this risk by ensuring that the intermediary service can only request service tickets for approved backend services, reducing the potential blast radius of an attack.

Another benefit of constrained delegation is that it aligns with the principle of least privilege. By limiting services to only those explicitly required for their operation, organizations reduce unnecessary exposure and improve their overall security posture. This approach also helps to comply with regulatory requirements that demand strict controls over how user credentials and identity tokens are handled and forwarded between services.

Constrained delegation is commonly used in web-based applications that require backend database or file server access. For example, a web server that provides reporting dashboards might need to query a backend SQL Server database on behalf of authenticated users. Through constrained delegation, administrators can permit the web server to delegate only to the SQL Server SPN, ensuring that the web server cannot misuse delegated credentials to access unrelated resources, such as email servers or file shares.

Despite its benefits, constrained delegation does introduce some administrative complexity. Properly configuring delegation policies requires careful identification of which backend services each intermediary service must access. Additionally, SPNs must be correctly registered in the Kerberos realm or directory service, as misconfigured or duplicate SPNs can cause authentication failures. Administrators must also monitor delegation usage, regularly auditing policies to ensure that permissions remain aligned with operational and security needs.

In environments where even greater control is required, organizations can opt for resource-based constrained delegation. This variant allows the backend service to define which intermediary services are allowed to delegate on behalf of users, rather than setting the policy at the intermediary service level. Resource-based constrained delegation is particularly useful in multi-domain or federated environments where backend services are administered separately from intermediary services.

From an operational perspective, constrained delegation works seamlessly with other Kerberos security mechanisms, including mutual authentication, time synchronization, and ticket expiration. When a backend service receives a delegated ticket, it verifies the ticket's integrity, decrypts it using its secret key, and checks that the session key and timestamps are valid. These steps ensure that both the intermediary service and the backend resource can trust the authenticity of the delegated credentials.

Constrained delegation is a vital tool for organizations that rely on Kerberos for secure authentication across distributed applications. By limiting the scope of delegation, it enables secure and efficient multi-tier authentication workflows while minimizing the risk of credential misuse. When combined with careful planning, proper configuration of SPNs, and regular policy audits, constrained delegation allows enterprises to enforce strong security boundaries while maintaining the flexibility required for modern application architectures. Its ability to safeguard delegated credentials while preserving user identity across complex service chains makes constrained delegation a key element of secure Kerberos deployments.

# Protocol Transition and Service for User to Self (S4U2Self)

Protocol Transition and Service for User to Self, commonly known as S4U2Self, is a key extension to the Kerberos authentication protocol. It was introduced to address scenarios where services need to obtain a Kerberos service ticket on behalf of a user, even when the user did not initially authenticate using Kerberos. This mechanism is particularly useful in hybrid environments where users might authenticate through non-Kerberos protocols, such as via a web form using a username and password, and the service still needs to operate in a Kerberos-secured environment by acquiring service tickets to downstream services on the user's behalf. S4U2Self is part of the broader Kerberos Service for User (S4U) framework, which was designed by Microsoft to solve limitations in traditional delegation and ticketing mechanisms.

The Protocol Transition element of S4U2Self allows a service that is trusted for delegation to request a Kerberos service ticket for a user who has not presented Kerberos credentials, effectively bridging authentication methods. For example, a user could authenticate to a web application using a non-Kerberos method such as a Secure Sockets Layer (SSL) client certificate or a basic authentication form. Without Protocol Transition, the web application would be unable to request Kerberos service tickets to backend systems on behalf of that user because no Kerberos Ticket Granting Ticket was issued. Protocol Transition solves this problem by allowing the service to use its own credentials to request a Kerberos ticket for the user, based solely on the user's identity.

The S4U2Self process begins when the service, having successfully authenticated the user via an alternative mechanism, contacts the Kerberos Key Distribution Center to request a service ticket as if the user had authenticated via Kerberos. The service presents its own service ticket, proving its identity and its authorization to perform delegation actions. The KDC validates that the service is configured for constrained delegation and that it is permitted to perform Protocol Transition on behalf of the specified user. If these conditions are met, the KDC issues a Kerberos service ticket representing the user, which the service can then use to access backend resources within the constraints defined by the delegation policy.

One of the key advantages of S4U2Self is that it enhances flexibility in multi-tier application architectures without requiring the user to be directly involved in Kerberos authentication. This capability is especially valuable in environments where not all users have Kerberos clients or where initial authentication occurs via protocols outside of Kerberos, such as Security Assertion Markup Language (SAML), OAuth, or other federated identity providers. The service's ability to transition the user into the Kerberos realm via S4U2Self preserves the benefits of Kerberos authentication, such as secure service tickets and mutual authentication, for subsequent resource access.

S4U2Self is tightly coupled with the concept of constrained delegation. Without constrained delegation enabled, a service would not have the necessary permissions to request a Kerberos ticket on behalf of the user. The KDC enforces this control by checking the delegation settings defined for the service principal. When combined with resource-based constrained delegation, S4U2Self becomes even more powerful and secure, as backend services gain control over which intermediary services are permitted to request tickets on behalf of users.

The workflow for S4U2Self consists of multiple steps. Initially, the user authenticates to the front-end service using a non-Kerberos protocol. Once the service receives the user's identity, it sends an S4U2Self request to the KDC along with its own valid service ticket. The KDC evaluates the request and, if successful, issues a forwardable service ticket for the user. The service can then either use this ticket directly to access backend resources on behalf of the user or proceed to the second stage of the S4U framework, which is S4U2Proxy. The S4U2Proxy step allows the service to request tickets to specific backend services, enabling complete multi-tier delegation.

Security is a critical consideration when deploying S4U2Self. To prevent misuse, only services explicitly configured and trusted for delegation are allowed to perform Protocol Transition. In Active Directory environments, administrators must configure the service account's properties to enable constrained delegation and select which services are eligible for delegation. This ensures that even if an attacker compromises a service account, they cannot freely impersonate users to all services within the domain, but only to those specifically authorized by policy.

S4U2Self is particularly useful in scenarios such as web single sign-on implementations, middleware services, and cloud-native applications that interact with on-premises Kerberos-secured resources. For example, a web portal that allows users to log in using external identity providers can leverage S4U2Self to obtain Kerberos tickets for users and access internal services such as SQL Server databases, file shares, or enterprise applications without requiring the user to present a Kerberos ticket during the initial login process.

Protocol Transition also supports modern hybrid identity solutions, where users may authenticate through cloud identity services and still require seamless access to Kerberos-protected resources hosted in on-premises data centers. By using S4U2Self, intermediary services such as application gateways or cloud-based web applications can bridge the gap between modern cloud authentication protocols and legacy Kerberos systems, supporting unified access control and identity propagation.

Administrators managing S4U2Self-enabled services must also monitor delegation-related logs and audit events closely. Windows-based environments, for instance, log delegation activities to the security event log, providing critical insight into when and how delegation is being used. Reviewing these logs regularly helps detect potential misuse or misconfiguration, such as services requesting tickets for unauthorized users or accessing backend systems outside of their delegation scope.

S4U2Self provides significant operational benefits, allowing organizations to extend Kerberos authentication to a wider range of applications and environments without compromising security. By combining the flexibility of protocol transition with the control of constrained delegation, Kerberos ensures that services can securely and efficiently act on behalf of users in scenarios where direct Kerberos authentication may not be possible or practical. This ability to enable secure identity propagation across varied systems has made S4U2Self an essential feature in many enterprise identity and access management architectures.

# S4U2Proxy and Resource Access

S4U2Proxy, or Service for User to Proxy, is a critical component of the Kerberos Service for User (S4U) extension that enables a service to obtain a Kerberos service ticket to another resource on behalf of a user. S4U2Proxy is designed to facilitate secure delegation in multi-tier application environments, where a service that has already authenticated a user needs to access additional backend services while maintaining the user's identity. It builds upon the capabilities of S4U2Self, where a service first obtains a service ticket representing the user, and then uses S4U2Proxy to gain access to specific resources downstream in the authentication chain.

The S4U2Proxy mechanism allows an intermediary service to present a user's existing service ticket to the Kerberos Ticket Granting Service and request a new service ticket for another service, effectively extending the user's authentication to subsequent systems without requiring the user to re-authenticate. This approach is vital for supporting Single Sign-On workflows and for enabling complex application architectures where intermediary services need to act on the user's behalf across different layers of the infrastructure. For example, when a user accesses a web application that, in turn, queries a SQL Server database, the web application can use S4U2Proxy to securely impersonate the user to the database server.

The S4U2Proxy process starts once the intermediary service, such as a web server, has obtained a user's service ticket either through direct Kerberos authentication or via S4U2Self in cases where the user originally authenticated using a non-Kerberos method. The service then forwards this ticket to the KDC's Ticket Granting Service along with a request to obtain a new service ticket for a specific backend service. The KDC validates the request by ensuring that the intermediary service is trusted for constrained delegation and that the requested backend service is one of the approved targets defined in the delegation policy. If the policy permits the request, the KDC issues a new service ticket that allows the intermediary service to connect to the backend system as if it were the user.

This delegated ticket is indistinguishable from a ticket that the user might have obtained directly. When the backend service receives this ticket, it sees the user's identity rather than that of the intermediary service. This enables the backend to enforce user-specific access controls, such as checking group memberships or applying role-based permissions. The backend service decrypts the ticket using its own service key, verifies the session key and the integrity of the ticket, and completes mutual authentication with the intermediary service.

S4U2Proxy is tightly integrated with constrained delegation, ensuring that services can only delegate access to explicitly approved resources. This security measure prevents a compromised intermediary service from impersonating users to arbitrary services within the Kerberos realm. Administrators configure these delegation permissions within directory services such as Microsoft Active Directory, where service accounts are granted permission to delegate to specific backend services. This fine-grained control is a key advantage of the S4U2Proxy model, as it mitigates the risks of credential misuse while still enabling seamless and secure delegation workflows.

One of the major use cases for S4U2Proxy is in multi-tier web applications. For example, a user might authenticate to an internal web portal, which then needs to retrieve data from an enterprise file server and a business intelligence application. Using S4U2Proxy, the web portal can request delegated tickets to both backend services without exposing the user to multiple login prompts or requiring separate Kerberos tickets to be obtained by the user. This seamless delegation preserves the Single Sign-On experience while ensuring that backend services enforce user-level security policies.

S4U2Proxy is also widely used in scenarios involving middleware or service brokers. In environments where an intermediary service routes or brokers requests between clients and multiple backend systems, S4U2Proxy allows the service to maintain the original user's identity context throughout the transaction chain. This is crucial for security, auditing, and compliance, as backend services log the true user identity rather than attributing actions to the intermediary service itself. The ability to preserve and propagate user identity using Kerberos tickets makes S4U2Proxy an essential part of enterprise-grade distributed applications.

The security of S4U2Proxy hinges on several key mechanisms. The forwardable flag in the user's original service ticket must be set, allowing the intermediary service to forward the ticket to the KDC. Additionally, time synchronization across all systems participating in the Kerberos realm is critical, as Kerberos tickets are time-sensitive and rely on synchronized clocks to prevent replay attacks. Furthermore, session keys associated with tickets must be securely managed to prevent unauthorized access to ticket contents and ensure the integrity of the authentication process.

S4U2Proxy also complements Kerberos' mutual authentication capabilities. When the intermediary service connects to the backend system using the delegated ticket, both parties perform mutual authentication using the session key derived from the Kerberos ticket. This ensures that both the intermediary service and the backend system can verify each other's identities, protecting against man-in-the-middle attacks and other forms of impersonation.

The flexibility of S4U2Proxy allows it to operate in both intradomain and cross-domain scenarios, provided that appropriate trust relationships are established between Kerberos realms or Active Directory domains. In cross-realm deployments, S4U2Proxy enables intermediary services to extend delegated authentication workflows beyond the boundaries of a single domain, supporting federated authentication models and multi-organizational collaborations.

Administrators must carefully manage S4U2Proxy configurations to balance security and functionality. It is important to define constrained delegation policies that limit intermediary services to only those backend systems required for business operations. Excessive delegation permissions increase the risk of misuse if a service account is compromised. Regular audits and reviews of delegation settings, service principal configurations, and key management practices are essential to maintaining a secure delegation environment.

S4U2Proxy has become a cornerstone in modern Kerberos deployments, providing the necessary delegation capabilities to support secure, scalable, and user-transparent access to resources across distributed networks. Whether enabling seamless access to backend databases, file systems, or enterprise applications, S4U2Proxy allows services to operate on behalf of users in a manner that preserves identity integrity and supports robust access control. Its integration with constrained delegation ensures that organizations can adopt complex application architectures without sacrificing security or control over how user credentials are used and propagated within the Kerberos trust model.

# Integrating Kerberos with LDAP

Integrating Kerberos with LDAP provides organizations with a powerful and scalable authentication and directory service solution. Kerberos handles secure authentication by providing a ticket-based system for verifying the identity of users and services, while LDAP, the Lightweight Directory Access Protocol, serves as the centralized directory service that stores user, group, and resource information. By combining these two technologies, organizations can create an environment where authentication and identity management are seamlessly linked, improving security, efficiency, and user experience. The integration of Kerberos and LDAP is common in enterprise environments, where centralized management and single sign-on capabilities are essential for controlling access to a wide variety of networked services.

At the heart of this integration is the division of responsibilities between Kerberos and LDAP. Kerberos focuses on the authentication process, verifying who a user or service claims to be. It does so by issuing and validating encrypted tickets that are used to access services securely. LDAP, on the other hand, acts as a centralized repository for identity-related data, including usernames, passwords, group memberships, email addresses, and other attributes that define how users and resources are organized within the enterprise. While Kerberos confirms a user's identity, LDAP provides the additional context needed to authorize access to services based on roles, groups, and policies.

One of the most common integration models involves using LDAP as the backend directory service for Kerberos. In this setup, Kerberos stores principal account information, including the cryptographic keys for users and services, in an LDAP directory rather than in a flat file database. By doing so, the organization benefits from LDAP's scalability, replication capabilities, and centralized management interface. This model simplifies the management of large Kerberos environments, as administrators can manage user accounts, service principals, and policies using familiar LDAP tools and workflows.

An example of this integration is MIT Kerberos configured with an OpenLDAP backend. In such a scenario, the Kerberos Key Distribution Center is configured to use LDAP as the principal database. The KDC communicates with the LDAP server using a secure connection, typically via LDAPS or STARTTLS, to ensure that sensitive information, such as encryption keys and ticket data, is protected during transmission. The LDAP directory schema is extended to include Kerberos-specific object classes and attributes, such as krbPrincipalName, krbPrincipalKey, and krbTicketPolicy, which are used to store and manage Kerberos-related information.

Integrating Kerberos with LDAP also enables a unified identity infrastructure, where a single set of credentials is used for both authentication and directory services. When a user logs into a workstation or application, Kerberos authenticates the user and provides a Ticket Granting Ticket. The same user can then use LDAP to query directory information or to perform directory-bound tasks, such as modifying their profile or retrieving information about other users or services, without the need to re-authenticate. This creates a seamless Single Sign-On experience that streamlines user interactions with network services while reducing the number of times credentials must be entered or stored.

LDAP integration also enhances security by centralizing user account management and password policies. In environments where Kerberos and LDAP are tightly integrated, password changes can be synchronized across both systems. For instance, when a user changes their password through an LDAP self-service portal, the change is propagated to the Kerberos principal stored in LDAP, ensuring consistency between authentication and directory services. Strong password policies, enforced at the LDAP level, automatically apply to Kerberos authentication as well, providing an additional layer of control.

In addition to user authentication, Kerberos and LDAP integration plays an important role in service authentication and authorization. Many network services, such as web servers, file servers, and application servers, rely on LDAP for retrieving access control lists and group memberships. When Kerberos is used for authentication, the service authenticates the client's Kerberos ticket, then queries LDAP to determine if the user has the appropriate permissions to access the requested resource. This combination of Kerberos for secure identity verification and LDAP for granular authorization decisions forms the foundation of many enterprise access control systems.

Another benefit of Kerberos and LDAP integration is the support for federated environments and cross-realm trust. Organizations that maintain multiple Kerberos realms and LDAP directories can use referrals, synchronization, and trust relationships to provide a unified user experience across domains. For example, users from one realm can access resources in another realm by leveraging Kerberos cross-realm authentication, while LDAP referrals or meta-directory services provide access to directory information across multiple LDAP instances.

Configuring Kerberos and LDAP integration requires careful attention to security best practices. Both systems must be configured to use secure communication channels. Kerberos relies on secure session keys and ticket encryption, while LDAP should be configured to enforce secure binding via LDAPS or STARTTLS to protect directory queries and updates. Administrators must also ensure proper access controls are applied to LDAP objects, limiting which systems and users can read or modify sensitive Kerberos-related data such as principal keys and password hashes.

Auditing and logging are important components of a secure integration. Both Kerberos and LDAP generate logs that record authentication events, directory queries, and administrative actions. Reviewing these logs helps detect suspicious behavior, such as repeated failed login attempts, unauthorized access to LDAP objects, or unusual ticket requests. Integrating Kerberos and LDAP logs into a centralized Security Information and Event Management system enhances the ability to monitor and respond to security incidents.

Kerberos and LDAP integration is also crucial for interoperability with other enterprise systems. Many directory-aware applications, including email platforms, identity management tools, and collaboration services, support LDAP queries natively. By integrating Kerberos authentication with these LDAP-based applications, organizations enable secure and efficient access control without duplicating user account information across multiple systems.

In large-scale deployments, LDAP's replication capabilities further enhance the scalability and availability of the Kerberos infrastructure. By replicating LDAP directories across multiple servers and geographic locations, organizations ensure that Kerberos authentication remains resilient and responsive, even in the face of server failures or network disruptions. Load balancing across LDAP replicas reduces query latency and distributes the load efficiently across the network.

The integration of Kerberos with LDAP creates a robust and centralized identity and authentication infrastructure capable of supporting the security and operational demands of modern enterprises. By leveraging Kerberos for secure ticket-based authentication and LDAP for directory services and authorization data, organizations benefit from a unified system that simplifies administration, enhances security, and provides a consistent and user-friendly experience across the entire network. This integration is foundational in enabling efficient and scalable identity management, supporting everything from basic login processes to advanced Single Sign-On capabilities across diverse environments.

# Kerberos and Network File System (NFS)

Kerberos and Network File System (NFS) integration is a widely adopted approach to securing file sharing across enterprise networks. NFS is a distributed file system protocol that allows users to access files over a network as if they were located on a local disk. Traditionally, NFS lacked strong authentication mechanisms, relying primarily on IP-based restrictions and trusting client-reported user IDs, which left it vulnerable to spoofing attacks and unauthorized access. To address these limitations, NFS can be integrated with Kerberos, providing a secure authentication framework that enforces identity verification, ensures data confidentiality, and guarantees integrity when clients and servers interact.

Kerberos enhances NFS security by adding an additional layer of authentication and access control to the file-sharing process. When a client accesses an NFS share, Kerberos ensures that both the client and the NFS server mutually authenticate each other using encrypted tickets and session keys. This eliminates the inherent trust assumptions of older NFS implementations and protects against impersonation attacks. With Kerberos in place, users must first authenticate to the Kerberos Key Distribution Center and obtain a valid Ticket Granting Ticket. The client then requests a service ticket specifically for the NFS service running on the target server. This service ticket, encrypted with the NFS server's secret key, serves as proof of the user's identity and is presented to the NFS server during the mount or file access process.

A key advantage of using Kerberos with NFS is the support for different security flavors that dictate how Kerberos authentication and encryption are applied to NFS traffic. These security flavors are defined as krb5, krb5i, and krb5p. The krb5 flavor provides authentication only, ensuring that both the client and server verify each other's identities using Kerberos tickets but leaving the actual file data unprotected beyond standard network protocols. The krb5i flavor adds integrity checking to the data transfer, using cryptographic checksums to prevent tampering with the data as it travels across the network. The most secure option, krb5p, provides both authentication and encryption, protecting the confidentiality of the data by encrypting file contents during transmission between the client and the NFS server.

These security flavors allow organizations to choose the level of protection that best aligns with their security policies and operational requirements. For example, an internal network where confidentiality is less of a concern might use krb5i to ensure data integrity, while sensitive environments handling confidential or regulated data may require krb5p to ensure full encryption of file traffic.

Implementing Kerberos-secured NFS requires careful configuration of both the NFS server and client systems. On the server side, administrators must create a Kerberos service principal for the NFS service, typically following the format nfs/hostname@REALM. The server then generates a keytab file containing the encrypted key for this principal, which is securely stored on the server to allow the NFS daemon to authenticate with the KDC. The server's exports file must also be updated to specify that Kerberos security flavors are required for specific shared directories, replacing the traditional sys option with sec=krb5, sec=krb5i, or sec=krb5p as appropriate.

On the client side, systems must be configured to operate as Kerberos clients, capable of obtaining and managing Kerberos tickets. Clients authenticate to the Kerberos realm to acquire a Ticket Granting Ticket and subsequently request a service ticket for the NFS server they wish to mount or access. The mount command is then executed with the appropriate security flavor, specifying the Kerberos-secured options to establish a trusted connection. Once mounted, the NFS share is available to the client, and Kerberos authentication is transparently applied to all file operations performed on the share.

The use of Kerberos with NFS significantly strengthens access control mechanisms. Instead of relying solely on traditional file permissions and client-side user IDs, the NFS server uses the information from the Kerberos ticket to verify the user's identity. This ensures that only authenticated users from trusted Kerberos realms can access the NFS shares, and unauthorized users without valid tickets are denied access. This is particularly useful in multi-user environments or shared networks, where enforcing secure and verifiable identity checks is critical.

Beyond improved authentication and encryption, Kerberos-secured NFS also facilitates centralized identity management and Single Sign-On capabilities. Users who log into their workstation and obtain a Kerberos TGT as part of the login process can seamlessly access NFS shares protected by Kerberos without needing to supply additional credentials. This integration simplifies workflows, reduces password fatigue, and enhances productivity by removing repetitive login prompts while maintaining strong security assurances.

Time synchronization is an essential requirement for successful Kerberos and NFS integration. Because Kerberos tickets are time-sensitive and include expiration timestamps, all participating systems—clients, servers, and the KDC—must maintain closely synchronized system clocks. If clock skew exceeds the allowable window, typically five minutes, ticket validation may fail, preventing users from mounting or accessing NFS shares. To avoid such issues, administrators must configure all systems to use a reliable time synchronization service such as Network Time Protocol.

Kerberos-secured NFS also supports cross-realm authentication scenarios. Organizations with multiple Kerberos realms can establish trust relationships between their realms, allowing users from one realm to securely access NFS shares in another realm without requiring separate credentials. This flexibility is useful in federated environments or during mergers and acquisitions, where different organizations may operate separate Kerberos infrastructures but need to share file resources securely.

While integrating Kerberos with NFS provides substantial security improvements, it also introduces some operational considerations. For example, the added encryption overhead of krb5p can impact performance, especially in high-throughput environments or networks with limited bandwidth. Administrators must carefully balance security and performance requirements when selecting which Kerberos security flavor to deploy. Additionally, managing service principals and keytab files for NFS servers adds a layer of administrative complexity, requiring regular key rotation and secure keytab storage to maintain the integrity of the authentication process.

Kerberos integration with NFS is a well-established best practice for securing network file sharing in enterprise environments. By combining the strong authentication and encryption capabilities of Kerberos with the robust file-sharing functionality of NFS, organizations can ensure that sensitive data remains protected as it traverses the network. This integration reduces the risks associated with unauthorized access, data interception, and identity spoofing, helping enterprises meet compliance requirements and security standards. As modern IT infrastructures continue to expand, Kerberos-secured NFS remains a key element of secure and efficient networked storage solutions across a wide range of industries.


# Kerberos in Unix/Linux Environments

Kerberos has long been a cornerstone of authentication in Unix and Linux environments, providing a trusted and secure method to verify user and service identities over potentially insecure networks. The adoption of Kerberos in these operating systems is rooted in its ability to deliver strong mutual authentication using symmetric key cryptography, minimizing the risk of credential exposure while supporting Single Sign-On (SSO) capabilities. In Unix and Linux infrastructures, Kerberos plays a central role in securing communications between users, applications, and services, offering an efficient and scalable solution for enterprise-grade network security.

In Unix and Linux systems, Kerberos is commonly used to authenticate users during login, secure remote shell sessions, and protect access to services such as NFS shares, databases, and HTTP-based applications. The integration of Kerberos into these environments is made possible through the Kerberos client libraries and utilities that are available in nearly all major Linux distributions and Unix variants. Tools like kinit, klist, kdestroy, and kvno are standard utilities that allow users and administrators to interact with the Kerberos infrastructure, manage tickets, and troubleshoot authentication flows.

When a user logs into a Unix or Linux system configured with Kerberos, the login process can be integrated with the Kerberos authentication system through PAM (Pluggable Authentication Modules). The PAM framework allows administrators to configure Kerberos as the preferred authentication mechanism, prompting the user to enter their credentials, which are then used to request a Ticket Granting Ticket from the Kerberos Key Distribution Center. Once the TGT is obtained, it is stored in the user's credential cache and can be used to access Kerberos-enabled services without additional login prompts, enabling SSO across the environment.

The configuration of Kerberos in Unix and Linux environments typically involves modifying the krb5.conf file, which serves as the primary configuration file for Kerberos clients. This file specifies crucial information, such as the default realm, the locations of the KDCs and administrative servers, preferred encryption types, ticket lifetime policies, and mappings between domain names and realms. Properly configuring the krb5.conf file is essential for ensuring that clients can correctly locate and communicate with the appropriate KDCs, as well as adhere to the security policies of the organization's Kerberos realm.

In addition to client configuration, Unix and Linux systems often serve as hosts for Kerberized services. Common examples include SSH servers, Apache HTTP servers, NFS servers, and PostgreSQL databases. These services are configured to use Kerberos authentication by registering service principals with the KDC and storing the corresponding keys in local keytab files. For instance, an SSH server on a host named server01.example.com would typically have a host principal of the form host/server01.example.com@EXAMPLE.COM registered in the KDC. The associated keytab file would then be securely stored on the server and referenced by the SSH daemon to validate incoming Kerberos tickets from clients.

One of the key benefits of using Kerberos in Unix and Linux environments is the enhanced security it provides for remote access protocols. Secure Shell (SSH), a widely used remote administration tool, supports Kerberos authentication through the GSSAPI mechanism. When configured, users can authenticate to SSH servers using Kerberos tickets rather than passwords, reducing the risk of password interception and brute-force attacks. The SSH client automatically forwards the user's Kerberos credentials to the server, which then verifies the ticket and establishes a secure session, benefiting from Kerberos' mutual authentication to protect against man-in-the-middle attacks.

Kerberos is also integral to securing file sharing in Unix and Linux systems. NFS version 4, for example, supports Kerberos for both authentication and encryption of file system operations. When combined with Kerberos security flavors such as krb5, krb5i, and krb5p, NFS ensures that access to network file systems is authenticated using Kerberos tickets and that data integrity and confidentiality are maintained during transfers. This approach replaces older and less secure NFS methods that relied solely on client-side user ID mapping and IP-based restrictions.

Kerberos plays a crucial role in protecting web-based services hosted on Unix and Linux servers as well. Web applications running on platforms such as Apache or Nginx can be integrated with Kerberos using modules like mod_auth_kerb or GSSAPI modules, enabling users to log in to protected web portals using Kerberos credentials. This enables Single Sign-On for intranet applications, where users authenticated to their workstation can seamlessly access internal web resources without being prompted for additional passwords.

Time synchronization is a vital consideration when deploying Kerberos in Unix and Linux environments. Because Kerberos relies on timestamps to validate ticket authenticity and protect against replay attacks, all systems participating in the Kerberos realm must maintain synchronized clocks. This is typically achieved through Network Time

Protocol (NTP) services, ensuring that clients, servers, and KDCs remain within the allowed time skew window, commonly set to five minutes. Failing to maintain proper time synchronization can result in ticket validation failures and disruptions in service availability.

In Unix and Linux environments, Kerberos is often integrated with directory services such as LDAP or Microsoft Active Directory to centralize identity management. By combining Kerberos authentication with LDAP-based user directories, organizations can simplify user account management, enforce consistent password policies, and streamline access control across a wide range of services. In Active Directory-integrated environments, Unix and Linux systems can join the AD domain using tools like realmd, SSSD, or Samba, enabling them to authenticate users using Kerberos and resolve user identities via LDAP.

For administrators, Kerberos simplifies auditing and compliance by providing clear logs of authentication events. Kerberos logs record ticket requests, successful and failed authentications, and service ticket exchanges. By integrating these logs with centralized logging and monitoring systems, administrators can maintain visibility over authentication activities, detect anomalies, and respond to potential security incidents.

Kerberos has become an indispensable component of security architectures in Unix and Linux environments. Its ability to provide secure, ticket-based authentication while supporting SSO and mutual authentication makes it a trusted solution for protecting sensitive data and services in distributed systems. As Unix and Linux platforms continue to serve as critical infrastructure in enterprise networks, Kerberos remains an essential tool for safeguarding authentication processes and ensuring the integrity of communication between users and services. Its flexibility, strong cryptographic foundations, and seamless integration with existing security frameworks make it a preferred choice for securing modern Unix and Linux-based systems.

# Kerberos in Windows Environments

Kerberos is the default authentication protocol in modern Windows environments, forming the backbone of secure identity verification within Active Directory domains. Since its adoption with the release of Windows 2000, Kerberos has replaced the older NTLM (NT LAN Manager) protocol as the preferred method for authenticating users, computers, and services across enterprise networks. By leveraging Kerberos, Windows provides a highly secure, scalable, and efficient way to manage authentication for thousands of users and devices operating within a centralized directory service. Its integration with Active Directory enhances not only security but also user convenience through Single Sign-On, allowing users to authenticate once and access multiple network resources without repeated credential prompts.

In Windows domains, every domain controller functions as a Kerberos Key Distribution Center, hosting both the Authentication Service and the Ticket Granting Service. This allows domain-joined clients and servers to interact seamlessly with the KDC during the authentication process. When a user logs into a Windows machine that is joined to an Active Directory domain, their credentials are used to request a Ticket Granting Ticket from the KDC. The KDC validates the user's identity and issues the TGT, which is then used by the client to request service tickets for accessing various resources throughout the domain.

The integration of Kerberos with Active Directory ensures that authentication is tightly coupled with directory services, where user and computer accounts, security groups, and policies are centrally managed. Each user account in Active Directory has an associated Kerberos principal, and domain controllers store the cryptographic keys required to generate and validate Kerberos tickets for these principals. This tight integration simplifies administrative tasks such as user provisioning, password management, and access control, while also supporting advanced features such as Group Policy enforcement.

Windows services and applications also make extensive use of Kerberos for secure authentication. Common services like file shares, printers, SQL Server databases, web applications running on IIS, and Exchange servers all leverage Kerberos to authenticate clients and establish secure sessions. Service Principal Names (SPNs) are a critical component of this process. SPNs are unique identifiers assigned to services within the domain, allowing the Kerberos Ticket Granting Service to issue tickets for specific services. Administrators must ensure that SPNs are correctly configured for services such as HTTP, MSSQLSvc, or CIFS, as misconfigured SPNs can lead to authentication issues or fallback to NTLM, which is less secure.

One of the key benefits of using Kerberos in Windows environments is the built-in support for Single Sign-On. Once a user has obtained a Ticket Granting Ticket, they can access multiple resources within the domain, such as shared folders, internal websites, or remote desktops, without being prompted to re-enter their password. This SSO functionality improves productivity and user experience by eliminating redundant authentication steps while maintaining high security through encrypted tickets and session keys.

Windows Kerberos implementations also support delegation, allowing services to act on behalf of users when accessing downstream services. Delegation is essential in multi-tier applications where, for example, a front-end web application needs to query a backend SQL Server on behalf of the user. Windows supports both unconstrained and constrained delegation models, as well as resource-based constrained delegation. These delegation options allow administrators to control how and where credentials are forwarded within the domain, providing the flexibility to enable secure multi-tier authentication workflows without exposing users to unnecessary risks.

Kerberos in Windows environments is closely tied to Group Policy, providing administrators with the ability to enforce policies related to ticket lifetimes, encryption types, pre-authentication requirements, and delegation permissions. Group Policy Objects can be used to configure settings such as maximum ticket lifetime, renewal limits, and which encryption algorithms are permitted for ticket generation. Modern Windows domains typically favor AES-based encryption for Kerberos tickets due to its strength and compliance with current security standards, though backward compatibility with older algorithms can be enabled if needed.

Time synchronization plays a vital role in the successful operation of Kerberos within Windows environments. Kerberos tickets include timestamps to prevent replay attacks, and the KDC and all domain-joined devices must maintain closely synchronized system clocks. The Windows Time Service (W32Time) is typically used in conjunction with NTP servers to ensure that time discrepancies do not exceed the allowable skew window, which by default is five minutes. Failure to maintain synchronized time across the domain can result in authentication failures, particularly during ticket validation steps.

Kerberos also underpins many advanced security features in Windows environments, such as smart card logon and certificate-based authentication. In smart card logon scenarios, users present a physical smart card and enter a PIN, which the system uses to authenticate the user and request a Kerberos ticket. This two-factor authentication method enhances security by combining something the user has (the smart card) with something they know (the PIN), leveraging Kerberos to issue the necessary tickets for domain access.

Windows Kerberos logs provide valuable insights into authentication events across the domain. Administrators can use Event Viewer to review Kerberos-related events, including ticket requests, ticket renewals, and authentication failures. These logs are critical for auditing user activity, identifying misconfigurations, and detecting suspicious behavior such as brute-force attempts or unauthorized ticket requests. Integrating Kerberos logs into centralized security information and event management systems allows organizations to correlate authentication data with other security events and improve their incident response capabilities.

In hybrid environments, where organizations integrate on-premises Active Directory with Azure Active Directory or other cloud-based identity providers, Kerberos remains essential for managing authentication within the local domain. Even as cloud adoption grows, many organizations continue to rely on Kerberos for secure authentication to legacy systems, file shares, and internal applications hosted in private data centers. Solutions like Azure AD Connect enable organizations to bridge their on-premises Kerberos infrastructure with cloud-based identity services, supporting a hybrid identity model.

Kerberos in Windows environments is also essential for interoperability with non-Windows systems. Unix and Linux servers can be configured to join a Windows Active Directory domain and use Kerberos for authentication, enabling cross-platform SSO across mixed environments. Tools like Samba and SSSD facilitate this integration, allowing Linux systems to authenticate to Active Directory KDCs and participate in Kerberos-secured communication with Windows-based services.

Kerberos continues to be a critical element of Microsoft's security architecture, delivering a robust and time-tested authentication framework that scales to meet the demands of enterprise networks. Its seamless integration with Active Directory, support for mutual authentication, delegation, and Single Sign-On, and its ability to secure communications across diverse services and applications make it indispensable for protecting modern Windows infrastructures. As organizations continue to modernize their networks, Kerberos remains foundational in ensuring the integrity and security of authentication workflows in Windows environments.

# Kerberos and Web Applications

Kerberos plays a significant role in securing web applications by providing strong authentication and enabling seamless Single Sign-On experiences. As web applications have become a core part of enterprise IT infrastructures, the need to secure HTTP-based services with reliable authentication protocols has increased. Kerberos, originally designed to secure network resources in distributed environments, has evolved to integrate effectively with modern web technologies, offering a solution that is both secure and user-friendly. By using Kerberos in conjunction with web applications, organizations can reduce the reliance on password-based authentication and minimize the risk of credential theft, while streamlining the user experience.

The integration of Kerberos into web applications is most commonly implemented through HTTP Negotiate authentication, which allows web browsers and web servers to perform mutual authentication based on Kerberos tickets. In this model, when a user accesses a protected web resource, the browser automatically requests a service ticket for the web server's HTTP service principal and includes the ticket in the HTTP request header using the SPNEGO (Simple and Protected GSSAPI Negotiation Mechanism) protocol. The web server then validates the ticket using its stored service key, typically held in a keytab file, and establishes a secure session with the client.

One of the most compelling features of using Kerberos for web authentication is the support for Single Sign-On. Once users have logged into their domain-joined workstation and obtained a Ticket Granting Ticket, their Kerberos credentials can be automatically used to authenticate to multiple web applications within the same realm without requiring them to re-enter their credentials. This seamless authentication flow reduces friction for users, eliminating repetitive login prompts while maintaining high levels of security through encrypted ticket exchanges and mutual authentication.

To enable Kerberos authentication on the web server side, the server must have a service principal registered in the Kerberos Key Distribution Center. For example, a web server running on host webapp.example.com would typically use an SPN such as HTTP/webapp.example.com@EXAMPLE.COM. The corresponding service key is exported to a keytab file, which is securely stored on the web server. Web servers like Apache HTTP Server, Nginx, and Microsoft Internet Information Services support Kerberos authentication through specialized modules or built-in configurations. Apache uses the mod_auth_kerb or mod_auth_gssapi modules to handle Kerberos authentication, while IIS integrates with Kerberos natively as part of Windows Integrated Authentication.

For browsers to support Kerberos authentication with web applications, additional configuration is often required. Most modern browsers, including Microsoft Edge, Google Chrome, and Mozilla Firefox, can be configured to support HTTP Negotiate authentication for trusted domains. In enterprise settings, administrators typically define group policies or configuration preferences to enable this functionality automatically. For example, browsers can be configured to automatically send Kerberos tickets when accessing intranet domains such as *.example.com, ensuring that users benefit from SSO without being prompted to log in manually.

Kerberos authentication is also used to protect sensitive APIs and RESTful services that power modern web applications. By securing APIs with Kerberos, developers ensure that backend services only accept requests from authenticated clients, significantly reducing the risk of unauthorized access and API abuse. In microservices architectures, Kerberos can serve as the foundational authentication mechanism that secures communication between individual services, particularly in environments where services span multiple servers or datacenters within a secured Kerberos realm.

A key security benefit of integrating Kerberos with web applications is the elimination of password exchange over the network. Instead of submitting plaintext passwords to the web server, the client presents a ticket issued by the trusted Kerberos Key Distribution Center. This reduces the surface area for credential theft, as sensitive information like passwords does not traverse the network after the initial workstation login. Additionally, Kerberos provides mutual authentication, meaning that the client can also verify the identity of the web server before exchanging any sensitive data, mitigating the risk of man-in-the-middle attacks.

Kerberos' ticketing system also provides robust session control. Service tickets issued to clients are time-limited, reducing the window of opportunity for attackers in case a ticket is intercepted. Furthermore, Kerberos tickets are encrypted using strong cryptographic algorithms, ensuring that they cannot be forged or tampered with by malicious actors. The combination of encrypted tickets, mutual authentication, and centralized key management via the KDC makes Kerberos a resilient choice for protecting web-based services against common authentication threats.

Integrating Kerberos with web applications does present challenges, particularly in cross-platform or hybrid environments. Applications running on Linux-based web servers must be carefully configured to interoperate with Kerberos realms, which are often managed within Microsoft Active Directory. Ensuring proper DNS resolution, consistent time synchronization, and correct SPN configurations is essential to avoid authentication failures. Additionally, applications must handle fallback mechanisms for clients that do not support Kerberos, such as external partners or users accessing the application from non-domain-joined devices. In such cases, web applications often provide alternative authentication options, such as basic authentication over HTTPS or federated login using protocols like SAML or OAuth.

Kerberos can also be combined with reverse proxies to secure access to backend web applications. A reverse proxy configured to support Kerberos authentication can act as a gateway, validating Kerberos tickets on behalf of backend applications that do not natively support Kerberos. This model allows legacy or third-party web applications to benefit from Kerberos-based SSO without requiring them to be modified. Tools such as Apache HTTPD or NGINX can serve as these proxies, handling Kerberos authentication upstream and forwarding requests to backend services after validating the client's identity.

Kerberos support for web applications extends beyond traditional on-premises environments. In hybrid cloud scenarios, organizations can integrate Kerberos-secured web applications with modern identity providers. By federating Active Directory with Azure AD or other cloud identity platforms, enterprises can enable SSO across both cloud-hosted and on-premises web applications while maintaining the use of Kerberos for internal resources. This hybrid approach preserves the security and efficiency of Kerberos within the corporate network while enabling external or remote access through modern identity federation techniques.

Overall, Kerberos has become an indispensable tool for securing web applications in enterprise environments. Its ability to provide strong authentication, mutual trust, and Single Sign-On aligns perfectly with the needs of modern organizations looking to protect web-based services without compromising usability. As organizations continue to expand their reliance on web applications, integrating Kerberos remains a critical component of building a secure, scalable, and user-friendly authentication infrastructure that protects sensitive data and streamlines access to business-critical systems.

# Kerberos with HTTP/Negotiate Authentication

Kerberos with HTTP/Negotiate authentication is a widely adopted method to secure web-based communications and applications by combining the robustness of Kerberos with the convenience of browser-integrated Single Sign-On functionality. The HTTP/Negotiate mechanism, often referred to as SPNEGO (Simple and Protected GSSAPI Negotiation Mechanism), provides a framework that allows web browsers and servers to negotiate authentication protocols transparently. Kerberos is typically the preferred protocol negotiated, although alternatives such as NTLM may be used as a fallback in some environments. The integration of Kerberos with HTTP/Negotiate authentication helps enterprises enforce secure, centralized authentication for their internal web applications and APIs, reducing the exposure of user credentials and supporting seamless access across a variety of services.

The HTTP/Negotiate authentication workflow begins when a client, such as a web browser, attempts to access a protected web resource hosted on a server that supports Kerberos authentication. The server responds with a 401 Unauthorized status and a WWW-Authenticate header containing the Negotiate token, indicating that it supports Negotiate authentication. At this point, the browser checks whether it is configured to use Kerberos for the requested domain and whether the user is logged into a Kerberos-secured environment, typically an Active Directory domain.

If the conditions are met, the browser automatically retrieves a Kerberos service ticket for the web application from the Key Distribution Center. The service ticket is obtained for the HTTP service principal associated with the fully qualified domain name of the server. For example, if the user is accessing https://intranet.example.com, the browser requests a Kerberos ticket for the principal HTTP/intranet.example.com@EXAMPLE.COM. Once the ticket is retrieved, it is inserted into the Authorization header of the next HTTP request to the server as part of the Negotiate token.

On the server side, the web server must be properly configured to accept and validate Kerberos tickets. The server uses a local keytab file containing the secret key associated with its HTTP service principal to decrypt the ticket presented by the client. Upon successful decryption and verification of the ticket, the web server establishes the authenticated session, granting the client access to the requested web resource. This process is transparent to the user, who is not prompted to enter credentials if a valid Kerberos ticket is available. Instead, the user benefits from a seamless Single Sign-On experience, where authentication to web applications occurs automatically in the background.

HTTP/Negotiate authentication with Kerberos is commonly implemented on web servers such as Apache HTTPD, Nginx, and Microsoft Internet Information Services. In Apache, modules like mod_auth_gssapi or mod_auth_kerb handle the GSSAPI and Kerberos ticket verification, while in IIS, Kerberos is integrated directly through Windows Integrated Authentication. The web server configuration must specify the Kerberos authentication mechanism and reference the correct keytab file for the HTTP service principal. Additionally, to ensure that browsers use Kerberos for HTTP/Negotiate authentication, administrators must configure browser settings or group policies that define trusted sites or domains for which Kerberos tickets should be automatically sent.

For example, in an enterprise environment, administrators can configure Google Chrome or Microsoft Edge to automatically use Kerberos when accessing internal domains like *.example.com. This setting is typically managed through group policies in Active Directory or through browser-specific configuration files. Mozilla Firefox requires explicit settings in its about:config interface, where administrators specify trusted domains and enable negotiation for Kerberos tickets. By defining these trusted domains, organizations ensure that Kerberos is only used for authorized internal resources, reducing the risk of inadvertently sending Kerberos tickets to external or untrusted servers.

One of the key security benefits of using Kerberos with HTTP/Negotiate authentication is that passwords are never sent across the network during the web authentication process. Instead, clients use Kerberos tickets that have been securely obtained and encrypted using the trusted Kerberos infrastructure. This reduces the risk of credential theft through network sniffing or man-in-the-middle attacks. Moreover, Kerberos' mutual authentication feature ensures that both the client and the server verify each other's identities, protecting users from connecting to rogue or impersonated servers.

HTTP/Negotiate authentication is particularly valuable in securing intranet web applications, enterprise portals, and internal APIs. In such environments, users typically authenticate to their workstation using Kerberos as part of a domain login process, and their session includes a Ticket Granting Ticket. The browser reuses this TGT to obtain additional service tickets for web applications, allowing users to access multiple services without being prompted for credentials repeatedly. This Single Sign-On functionality improves user productivity and minimizes the need for password management, while maintaining robust security through Kerberos' ticketing system.

Kerberos with HTTP/Negotiate authentication can also be extended to protect RESTful APIs and backend services. Applications that expose APIs to internal clients or other services within the same Kerberos realm can leverage the same mechanism to ensure that all requests are authenticated using Kerberos tickets. This approach helps secure machine-to-machine communications in distributed systems, where automated processes and services interact with protected web APIs without embedding passwords or API keys.

Despite its benefits, configuring Kerberos with HTTP/Negotiate authentication requires careful attention to infrastructure and service configuration. Both the client and server systems must be correctly configured to participate in the Kerberos realm, including DNS resolution, time synchronization, and service principal registration. SPNs must be unique and properly assigned to the appropriate server accounts, as duplicate or misconfigured SPNs can cause authentication failures or force clients to fallback to less secure authentication mechanisms.

Another common challenge is managing cross-realm or federated authentication scenarios. In large organizations with multiple Kerberos realms or trusted domains, HTTP/Negotiate authentication can support cross-realm ticketing, allowing users from one realm to access web applications hosted in another realm. This requires careful management of cross-realm trust relationships and proper configuration of client and server realms to recognize and validate tickets from trusted external realms.

To further enhance security, some organizations deploy reverse proxies or load balancers that handle Kerberos ticket validation on behalf of backend applications. In this architecture, the reverse proxy performs HTTP/Negotiate authentication with clients and then forwards authenticated requests to backend services. This offloads the burden of Kerberos validation from individual web applications and centralizes authentication logic at the proxy layer. Tools such as Apache HTTPD, NGINX, or Microsoft's Application Proxy can be configured in this role, improving scalability and simplifying the authentication model for backend applications that may not natively support Kerberos.

HTTP/Negotiate authentication with Kerberos has become a standard approach for securing enterprise web applications due to its ability to deliver both strong security and a frictionless user experience. By leveraging the existing Kerberos infrastructure and extending it to HTTP-based services, organizations achieve centralized authentication, reduced credential exposure, and seamless access to critical internal resources. As enterprise environments continue to rely heavily on web technologies, integrating Kerberos through the HTTP/Negotiate framework remains a vital strategy for ensuring secure, efficient, and scalable web authentication across distributed systems.

# Kerberos and Cloud Integration

Kerberos and cloud integration have become increasingly important as organizations transition from traditional on-premises IT infrastructures to hybrid and fully cloud-based environments. Kerberos, originally designed to secure authentication within local networks, has adapted to modern architectures by integrating with cloud platforms and identity providers, enabling secure authentication and identity federation across hybrid ecosystems. While Kerberos remains foundational in protecting internal resources and applications, its integration with cloud services allows organizations to extend trusted authentication models beyond their local networks, providing users with secure and seamless access to both on-premises and cloud-hosted applications.

At the core of this integration is the need to bridge the identity and authentication gap between legacy on-premises Kerberos realms and modern cloud identity systems such as Azure Active Directory, AWS IAM Identity Center, or Google Cloud Identity. Many enterprises rely on Active Directory, which natively supports Kerberos, to manage user accounts and authentication within internal networks. As these organizations adopt cloud services, they face the challenge of maintaining a consistent and secure authentication framework while enabling cloud-native applications and services to interact with existing Kerberos-based systems.

One common approach to integrating Kerberos with the cloud is through directory synchronization and federation services. For example, Microsoft's Azure AD Connect allows organizations to synchronize their on-premises Active Directory, including its Kerberos-enabled authentication framework, with Azure Active Directory. This synchronization enables users to authenticate once within the on-premises Kerberos realm and gain access to cloud resources using Single Sign-On. When users log into their domain-joined machines and receive a Kerberos Ticket Granting Ticket, Azure AD Connect federates that authentication with Azure AD, allowing users to access Microsoft 365 services, SaaS applications, and custom cloud-hosted applications without re-authenticating.

Another model is to integrate Kerberos-secured applications with cloud-based reverse proxies or identity brokers. For example, a company may deploy Microsoft Azure AD Application Proxy or another identity-aware reverse proxy that accepts Kerberos authentication from internal clients and forwards those identities to cloud-hosted applications. In this architecture, users inside the corporate network authenticate to the proxy using Kerberos tickets, and the proxy then translates that identity into a token or assertion understood by the cloud service, such as a SAML assertion or OAuth

2.0 access token. This allows internal Kerberos authentication to be leveraged for cloud-hosted web applications, preserving security while simplifying the user experience.

Kerberos cloud integration is also vital for hybrid access to legacy applications that cannot be easily migrated to the cloud. Many enterprises operate critical applications that rely on Kerberos for secure authentication but also require these applications to be accessible to remote users or services hosted in the cloud. Through solutions like Azure Active Directory Federation Services (AD FS) or custom Security Token Services, organizations can issue tokens to cloud-based users or applications, granting them access to Kerberos-protected resources hosted on-premises. These tokens act as intermediaries, allowing cloud-native services to operate within the security boundaries of the Kerberos realm without direct access to Kerberos tickets or keys.

Cloud providers have also developed solutions to support Kerberos-based authentication in their virtualized environments. For example, Amazon Web Services offers Managed Microsoft AD and AWS Directory Service, allowing organizations to deploy fully managed Active Directory-compatible domains in the cloud. These services provide Kerberos authentication for EC2 instances, Amazon FSx file systems, and other AWS resources, enabling organizations to extend Kerberos authentication to cloud workloads while retaining the familiar administration model of Active Directory. Similarly, Google Cloud's Managed Microsoft AD allows organizations to integrate Kerberos into Google Cloud-hosted applications and virtual machines, providing secure authentication and centralized identity management.

Containerized and microservices-based architectures also benefit from Kerberos integration with cloud-native platforms. Applications running in Kubernetes clusters, for instance, may still need to authenticate to on-premises Kerberos-secured services such as databases, file servers, or APIs. This can be achieved by securely mounting Kerberos keytab files into application pods and configuring Kerberos clients within containers to interact with the organization's KDC or Active Directory domain controllers. This integration allows cloud-native applications to securely access legacy resources using

Kerberos tickets, maintaining interoperability across the hybrid infrastructure.

An important aspect of Kerberos cloud integration is the continued reliance on secure communication and strict key management. When extending Kerberos into the cloud, organizations must ensure that KDCs or domain controllers are securely accessible to cloud workloads. This often involves establishing VPNs, ExpressRoute connections, or other private networking solutions that securely bridge on-premises data centers and cloud environments. Additionally, time synchronization remains critical, as Kerberos relies on accurate timestamps for ticket validation. All systems, whether on-premises or cloud-hosted, must maintain synchronized clocks, typically through Network Time Protocol, to prevent ticket expiration and replay attack vulnerabilities.

From a security perspective, integrating Kerberos with cloud environments introduces additional considerations. Administrators must carefully manage cross-realm trust relationships, federation configurations, and service principal management to ensure that only authorized entities can participate in Kerberos ticket exchanges. Moreover, integrating Kerberos with cloud services should be coupled with strong monitoring and auditing processes, as organizations must detect and respond to anomalies such as unauthorized ticket requests, failed delegations, or suspicious ticket forwarding activity.

Another area of growing interest is the integration of Kerberos with Zero Trust security models. While Kerberos traditionally operates within trusted network boundaries, modern security architectures advocate for continuous verification of identity and device posture, regardless of location. Cloud-based identity providers can complement Kerberos authentication by layering additional context-aware access controls, such as conditional access policies, multi-factor authentication, and device compliance checks. In this model, Kerberos continues to secure internal authentication workflows, while cloud-based identity solutions enforce dynamic access policies based on risk signals and security posture.

Kerberos integration with cloud services also plays a role in supporting DevOps and automation practices. Automated processes running in cloud environments often require secure access to Kerberos-protected resources, such as source code repositories, internal APIs, or shared file systems. By securely provisioning keytab files, managing service principals, and integrating Kerberos authentication into CI/CD pipelines, organizations can maintain secure automated workflows across hybrid environments. This ensures that even automated services follow the same secure authentication practices as human users.

As organizations accelerate their digital transformation initiatives, the integration of Kerberos with cloud environments continues to be a critical component of hybrid identity strategies. By enabling secure authentication across both on-premises and cloud-based systems, Kerberos provides continuity, security, and efficiency for enterprises navigating complex IT landscapes. Whether supporting legacy applications, enabling modern web services, or securing hybrid workloads, Kerberos remains a trusted authentication standard, evolving to meet the demands of cloud-integrated architectures while preserving its core principles of strong cryptography, mutual authentication, and centralized ticket management.

# Kerberos in Hybrid Environments

Kerberos in hybrid environments represents a critical component of modern enterprise security strategies, as organizations increasingly operate infrastructures that span both on-premises data centers and cloud platforms. A hybrid environment typically combines legacy systems and applications, which rely on Kerberos for secure authentication within private networks, with cloud-based services and applications that may use modern identity protocols like SAML, OAuth, or OpenID Connect. The challenge for many organizations is to integrate Kerberos into this hybrid model while maintaining consistent security, supporting seamless user experiences, and ensuring interoperability between on-premises and cloud resources.

The primary strength of Kerberos in hybrid environments is its ability to provide strong mutual authentication and Single Sign-On for internal systems, even as organizations expand their workloads to cloud services. Kerberos continues to function as the trusted authentication backbone for domain-joined devices and users accessing on-premises resources, such as file servers, databases, and internal web applications. Users log into their corporate devices, receive a Kerberos Ticket Granting Ticket from the Key Distribution Center, and use this ticket to access various internal services without needing to repeatedly enter credentials. This internal authentication model remains unchanged in hybrid environments, reinforcing Kerberos as a foundation for internal trust.

The hybrid complexity emerges when these same users need to access cloud-hosted applications or when cloud-native services need to authenticate to on-premises Kerberos-protected resources. Bridging this gap often requires identity federation between the on-premises Kerberos realm, typically represented by Active Directory, and cloud identity platforms such as Azure Active Directory, AWS Identity Center, or Google Cloud Identity. Federation enables users who have authenticated via Kerberos to be granted access tokens or assertions that are accepted by cloud-based applications, maintaining secure access without duplicating identity stores or requiring separate logins.

One common approach is the use of synchronization tools like Azure AD Connect, which synchronizes user identities and group memberships from the on-premises Active Directory to Azure Active Directory. While Kerberos handles authentication within the local network, Azure AD Connect enables those same users to be recognized in the cloud. When users attempt to access SaaS applications integrated with Azure AD, their identity is federated through mechanisms like Active Directory Federation Services or directly through Azure AD's integrated Kerberos support, which can validate Kerberos tokens and issue cloud-compatible tokens for web applications and services.

Hybrid environments often require secure, bi-directional communication between cloud workloads and on-premises Kerberos-secured services. For example, a cloud-hosted web application might need to authenticate to an on-premises SQL Server database that relies on Kerberos for secure access. In such cases, organizations establish secure network connections, such as VPNs or dedicated private links like Azure ExpressRoute or AWS Direct Connect, to extend the trusted boundary between the cloud and the corporate network. Within this secure network extension, the cloud workload, often running in a virtual machine or container, is configured with Kerberos client libraries and a service principal keytab to authenticate to the on-premises KDC.

Administrators must also manage service principal names and keytab files carefully in hybrid models, ensuring that cloud-hosted services are registered with the appropriate Kerberos principals in the on-premises realm. These services then use Kerberos tickets to securely access protected resources inside the data center, preserving the same level of security as on-premises applications. The ability to extend Kerberos authentication across cloud boundaries allows organizations to modernize their application delivery models while continuing to leverage their existing Kerberos-secured assets.

Single Sign-On remains a critical driver for integrating Kerberos into hybrid environments. When properly configured, users can log into their corporate devices, authenticate once using Kerberos, and seamlessly access both internal applications and federated cloud services. For example, users might access an internal HR portal protected by Kerberos, followed by cloud-hosted Microsoft 365 applications like SharePoint Online or Outlook on the web, without re-authenticating. Federation services convert the Kerberos-authenticated session into SAML or OpenID Connect tokens that are accepted by the cloud applications, delivering a unified and efficient authentication experience.

Hybrid environments also introduce delegation scenarios where cloud-based services need to act on behalf of users within the on-premises Kerberos realm. Using Kerberos delegation techniques such as constrained delegation or resource-based constrained delegation, organizations can allow trusted cloud services to obtain service tickets on behalf of users to access legacy applications or data repositories hosted internally. This capability is vital for cloud-native applications that must integrate with older, Kerberos-protected APIs, file shares, or databases that cannot be easily migrated to the cloud.

Security considerations in hybrid Kerberos environments are paramount. The expansion of the Kerberos trust model beyond the internal network introduces new attack surfaces that must be carefully mitigated. Administrators must ensure that all participating systems, whether on-premises or in the cloud, maintain synchronized clocks using Network Time Protocol to prevent ticket validation errors and replay attacks. Secure encryption algorithms, such as AES-256, should be enforced for Kerberos tickets, and service principals should be managed with strict policies around key rotation and access control.

Monitoring and auditing are equally important. Kerberos authentication logs should be centralized and correlated with cloud-native logging systems to detect anomalies, such as unauthorized ticket requests from cloud services or suspicious patterns of cross-realm authentication. Combining Kerberos logs with Security Information and Event Management (SIEM) platforms enables security teams to gain end-to-end visibility across hybrid authentication workflows.

As organizations continue adopting Zero Trust principles, Kerberos plays a role in supporting internal authentication workflows while external access is governed by cloud-based conditional access policies. In hybrid Zero Trust architectures, Kerberos may still authenticate users to internal resources, but access to cloud applications is augmented by additional signals such as device compliance, geolocation, or multi-factor authentication enforced by cloud identity providers.

Hybrid environments may also leverage modern solutions like Azure AD Kerberos for Azure Files, which allows domain-joined virtual machines in Azure to authenticate to Azure Files using native Kerberos. This reduces the reliance on legacy authentication methods and simplifies file share access in cloud-native workloads. Similarly, hybrid identity solutions enable organizations to deploy managed Kerberos realms in the cloud, such as AWS Managed Microsoft AD, that integrate with on-premises realms to create a federated and unified identity plane.

Kerberos in hybrid environments is a powerful bridge between the stability of traditional authentication models and the flexibility of cloud adoption. Its integration into hybrid architectures ensures that enterprises can continue to rely on trusted Kerberos workflows while enabling seamless interaction with modern cloud services and applications. By carefully managing trust relationships, configuring federation services, and maintaining strong security controls, organizations can deploy Kerberos as a foundational component of secure, hybrid enterprise environments.

# Common Vulnerabilities in Kerberos

Kerberos is widely regarded as a robust and secure authentication protocol, but like any complex security system, it is not immune to vulnerabilities. Many of the weaknesses in Kerberos stem not from the protocol itself, but from how it is implemented, configured, and maintained in real-world environments. Understanding these common vulnerabilities is essential for system administrators, security teams, and organizations that rely on Kerberos to safeguard access to critical resources. When improperly configured or neglected, Kerberos systems can become vulnerable to attacks that undermine the security of the authentication process and expose sensitive information.

One of the most well-known vulnerabilities associated with Kerberos is the Pass-the-Ticket attack. In this scenario, an attacker who gains access to a valid Kerberos ticket, typically by compromising a workstation or intercepting the ticket from memory, can reuse that ticket to impersonate the legitimate user across the network. Since Kerberos tickets are often valid for several hours, attackers have a significant window of opportunity to exploit compromised tickets. The Pass-the-Ticket attack is particularly dangerous when it involves Ticket Granting Tickets, as these tickets allow attackers to request additional service tickets from the Ticket Granting Service without needing the user's password.

A related threat is the Pass-the-Key attack, where an attacker steals a user's session key or a service's secret key from memory or insecure storage. With this key, the attacker can forge or manipulate Kerberos tickets, potentially bypassing normal authentication workflows. Both Pass-the-Ticket and Pass-the-Key attacks highlight the importance of endpoint security, as attackers typically require access to a system's memory or file system to extract these valuable artifacts. Organizations should prioritize securing client devices and servers by enforcing strong system hardening practices and limiting privileged access.

Another critical vulnerability in Kerberos systems is the Golden Ticket attack. A Golden Ticket is a forged Ticket Granting Ticket created by an attacker who has compromised the Kerberos Key Distribution Center's master key, also known as the krbtgt account key. With this master key, the attacker can create TGTs for any user or service within the Kerberos realm, effectively granting themselves unrestricted access across the entire domain. The Golden Ticket attack is particularly devastating because it allows attackers to operate with stealth, bypassing standard logging and monitoring mechanisms. Defending against Golden Ticket attacks requires strong protection of domain controllers, regular rotation of the krbtgt account password, and comprehensive auditing to detect unusual ticket activity.

Silver Ticket attacks are another variation of ticket forgery that target individual service tickets instead of the TGT. In a Silver Ticket attack, an attacker with access to a service's key, often obtained from a compromised keytab file or memory dump, can forge a valid service ticket for that specific service. This allows the attacker to authenticate to the service without interacting with the KDC, making detection more difficult. Silver Ticket attacks are typically used to access services such as SQL Server or web applications, where the attacker can escalate privileges or exfiltrate data once inside.

Kerberos is also vulnerable to brute-force and password spraying attacks against the pre-authentication step. During the initial Authentication Service request, the KDC checks whether the user has provided a valid encrypted timestamp using their secret key. If pre-authentication is enabled, this step mitigates the risk of offline brute-force attacks. However, in environments where pre-authentication is disabled for specific accounts, attackers can request and capture an encrypted AS-REP response without providing a valid password. The attacker can then attempt to brute-force the password offline, leveraging tools such as ASREPRoast. Ensuring that pre-authentication is enforced for all user accounts is a critical security control to prevent this class of attack.

Kerberoasting is another prevalent attack technique that exploits how service principal keys are used in Kerberos. In this attack, an attacker requests a service ticket for a Kerberos-enabled service, captures the ticket encrypted with the service's key, and attempts to brute-force the key offline. If the service account has a weak or poorly managed password, the attacker may recover the password and use it to impersonate the service or escalate privileges. Service accounts with elevated rights, such as those used for databases or critical applications, are especially attractive targets for Kerberoasting. Organizations should mitigate this risk by enforcing strong, complex passwords for all service accounts, limiting unnecessary privileges, and rotating service account credentials regularly.

Trust relationships in cross-realm authentication scenarios also introduce vulnerabilities. If an organization establishes a Kerberos trust with another domain or realm that has weaker security controls, an attacker who compromises the less secure realm could potentially exploit the trust to access resources in the more secure realm. This risk is amplified in environments where transitive trusts are configured without thorough vetting of the security posture of the connected realms. Security teams must carefully review and audit cross-realm trust relationships to ensure that only trusted and well-secured domains are interconnected.

Time synchronization issues are another source of vulnerability in Kerberos environments. Kerberos relies on timestamp validation to prevent replay attacks and ensure ticket freshness. If the clocks of clients, servers, or KDCs are not synchronized, legitimate tickets may be rejected, or attackers may exploit the time discrepancy to replay previously captured tickets. Enforcing strict time synchronization using Network Time Protocol across all systems in the Kerberos realm is vital to maintaining the integrity of the ticketing system.

Weak encryption configurations also pose risks to Kerberos security. Older encryption types such as DES or RC4 are susceptible to cryptographic attacks and should be disabled in favor of modern algorithms like AES-128 or AES-256. Kerberos realms that continue to support deprecated encryption types risk exposing tickets and session keys to cracking attempts. Administrators must review their Kerberos configuration files and Active Directory settings to enforce the use of strong encryption across all ticket exchanges.

In addition to these technical vulnerabilities, human factors such as misconfigured service principals, improperly managed keytab files, and insufficient logging can weaken Kerberos security. Service principals should be carefully registered with unique and descriptive names to avoid SPN duplication, which can lead to authentication failures or unauthorized access. Keytab files containing service keys must be protected with strict file permissions, as unauthorized access to these files can result in Silver Ticket attacks.

Kerberos remains a powerful and effective authentication protocol, but organizations must be vigilant in addressing its common vulnerabilities. By implementing security best practices, including regular key rotations, hardening endpoint security, enforcing strong password policies, and auditing ticket usage, enterprises can significantly reduce the risk of Kerberos-based attacks. A layered defense strategy, combined with continuous monitoring and incident response readiness, is essential to protecting the integrity of Kerberos authentication systems in today's evolving threat landscape.

# Pass-the-Ticket and Pass-the-Hash Attacks

Pass-the-Ticket and Pass-the-Hash attacks are two of the most prominent credential-based attack techniques targeting enterprise networks, particularly in environments that rely on Kerberos and NTLM authentication protocols. Both techniques allow attackers to impersonate legitimate users and escalate privileges without directly knowing the user's password. Instead, they leverage authentication artifacts such as Kerberos tickets or NTLM password hashes obtained from compromised systems. These attacks highlight weaknesses in how credentials and session tokens are handled and stored on endpoints, making them a critical focus for cybersecurity professionals working to protect enterprise infrastructures.

Pass-the-Ticket attacks exploit the Kerberos ticketing system. In a typical Kerberos authentication flow, users authenticate to the Key

Distribution Center and receive a Ticket Granting Ticket, which is then used to request service tickets for accessing specific network resources. These tickets are stored in memory within the user's session. If an attacker gains access to a machine where a Kerberos-authenticated session is active, they can extract the cached tickets directly from system memory using tools such as Mimikatz. Once extracted, these tickets can be injected into another session on the same or a different machine, allowing the attacker to impersonate the original user and access services that trust the stolen ticket.

Pass-the-Ticket is particularly dangerous because the attacker does not need to compromise the user's password. Instead, the ticket itself, which includes encrypted session keys and identity assertions, becomes the token for lateral movement within the network. Since service tickets can be valid for hours and Ticket Granting Tickets may be renewable, attackers may have an extended window of opportunity to move laterally and access additional resources. When combined with Kerberos delegation mechanisms, such as unconstrained or constrained delegation, Pass-the-Ticket attacks can also allow attackers to escalate their privileges by impersonating users to sensitive backend systems like databases or file shares.

Pass-the-Hash attacks, on the other hand, target the NTLM authentication protocol. NTLM is still widely supported in enterprise networks for backward compatibility, especially in mixed environments that include legacy systems. In an NTLM authentication scenario, the user's password is hashed using a cryptographic function, and this hash is used to authenticate against remote systems without sending the actual password over the network. Pass-the-Hash attacks take advantage of this by allowing attackers to capture and reuse these password hashes directly. Once an attacker has obtained a valid NTLM hash, they can use it to authenticate to other systems without needing to know the plaintext password.

Like Pass-the-Ticket attacks, Pass-the-Hash exploits cached or stored credentials on compromised machines. Attackers can extract NTLM hashes from memory, Security Accounts Manager (SAM) databases, or through network captures during authentication processes. After obtaining the hash, tools like psexec, smbexec, or specially crafted scripts can be used to authenticate to other networked systems, often leading to lateral movement across domain-joined devices. In Windows environments, where NTLM is commonly used for local administrator accounts or legacy services, Pass-the-Hash can be particularly effective for expanding an attacker's footprint within the network.

Both attack techniques are frequently used as part of a broader strategy in Advanced Persistent Threat campaigns. Attackers often begin by compromising a low-privileged account or system and then leverage Pass-the-Ticket or Pass-the-Hash to escalate privileges and gain access to higher-value targets, such as domain controllers, file servers, or executive workstations. In cases where attackers obtain Kerberos tickets for privileged accounts or NTLM hashes for accounts with administrative rights, they can effectively control entire network segments.

A key enabler of both attack types is poor endpoint security hygiene. Systems with outdated software, weak configurations, or lax administrative controls are more susceptible to credential dumping. Additionally, shared accounts, local administrator accounts with identical passwords across multiple systems, and long-lived service accounts with static credentials provide attackers with multiple opportunities to harvest reusable authentication artifacts.

Defending against Pass-the-Ticket and Pass-the-Hash attacks requires a multi-layered approach. For Pass-the-Ticket, organizations must ensure that Kerberos tickets and credential caches are protected. Limiting the use of unconstrained delegation, enforcing short ticket lifetimes, and requiring mutual authentication between clients and services are essential defensive measures. Regularly clearing cached tickets when no longer needed, combined with session timeouts, can reduce the risk of stolen tickets being used for prolonged lateral movement.

For Pass-the-Hash mitigation, organizations should limit or eliminate the use of NTLM where possible, transitioning to Kerberos or other modern authentication protocols. Ensuring that each system has unique local administrator passwords, for example, through Local Administrator Password Solution (LAPS), helps reduce the impact of harvested hashes. Credential Guard, a security feature in Windows, helps protect NTLM hashes and Kerberos tickets by isolating them in a secure, virtualized environment, preventing attackers from dumping them from memory.

Network segmentation plays a significant role in limiting the effectiveness of these attacks. By isolating critical infrastructure, such as domain controllers or sensitive file servers, from general workstation networks, organizations can prevent attackers from moving laterally as easily using stolen tickets or hashes. Implementing firewall rules, application whitelisting, and privileged access management further reduces the pathways available to attackers.

Monitoring and detection are crucial. Both Pass-the-Ticket and Pass-the-Hash attacks leave traces in security logs that can be correlated to identify suspicious activity. For example, security teams can monitor for unusual Kerberos ticket usage, such as tickets being used from unexpected machines or outside of normal working hours. Similarly, detecting NTLM authentications that originate from compromised or unusual sources can help identify a Pass-the-Hash attempt. Integrating Kerberos and NTLM event logs into a centralized SIEM system allows for better correlation and faster incident response.

Another critical component of defense is limiting the exposure of privileged accounts. Admin accounts should never be used to log into non-secure or lower-privileged machines, as this practice exposes sensitive credentials to potential theft. Instead, privileged users should follow tiered access models, where administrative activities are performed only from secure, hardened systems designed for that purpose.

Pass-the-Ticket and Pass-the-Hash attacks continue to pose a significant risk to enterprise networks due to their ability to bypass traditional authentication processes and facilitate rapid lateral movement. By understanding the mechanics behind these attacks and implementing strong technical and procedural defenses, organizations can reduce the likelihood of successful credential-based attacks and strengthen their overall security posture. These attacks serve as a reminder that protecting authentication artifacts is as important as safeguarding passwords, and that securing endpoints and identities must be a top priority in any modern cybersecurity strategy.

# Golden Ticket and Silver Ticket Attacks

Golden Ticket and Silver Ticket attacks represent two of the most advanced and dangerous threats targeting Kerberos-secured environments. Both techniques are based on forging Kerberos tickets to bypass authentication mechanisms and gain unauthorized access to resources within a Windows Active Directory or other Kerberos-based environments. While both attacks exploit weaknesses in how Kerberos tickets are issued and validated, they differ in scope and impact, with Golden Tickets allowing complete control over a domain and Silver Tickets providing targeted access to specific services. Understanding these attack vectors is crucial for any organization that relies on Kerberos for authentication and wants to protect itself against credential forgery and privilege escalation.

A Golden Ticket attack involves forging a Ticket Granting Ticket (TGT), which is the core component of the Kerberos authentication process. The TGT is issued by the Key Distribution Center's Authentication Service and allows users to request service tickets for resources throughout the domain. In a Golden Ticket attack, an attacker must first compromise the Kerberos service account known as krbtgt, which holds the master key used to sign all TGTs in the domain. This key is critical to the entire Kerberos trust model, as all domain controllers within the realm rely on it to validate the authenticity of TGTs presented by clients.

Once an attacker has obtained the krbtgt account's password hash, typically through credential dumping techniques on a compromised domain controller, they can create fully forged TGTs. These forged tickets are indistinguishable from legitimate ones to any service or system within the domain because they are signed with the legitimate krbtgt key. This gives the attacker the ability to impersonate any user, including domain administrators, and request service tickets for any resource within the domain. The attacker can also manipulate ticket attributes, such as the ticket's lifetime, permissions, or group memberships, granting themselves unrestricted access to critical systems and data.

The Golden Ticket attack is considered one of the most severe threats because it effectively grants attackers the ability to become any user in the domain and persist indefinitely until the krbtgt key is rotated. Attackers can move laterally across the network, access sensitive files, modify Active Directory configurations, and execute commands on remote systems, all without triggering standard authentication or authorization alarms. Since the attacker no longer needs to interact with the KDC to request tickets, detecting Golden Ticket usage requires vigilant monitoring of anomalous activity patterns and ticket attributes.

Silver Ticket attacks are similar in that they involve forging Kerberos tickets, but they specifically target service tickets instead of TGTs. Service tickets, or Ticket Granting Service (TGS) tickets, are issued by the KDC when a client presents a TGT and requests access to a specific service, such as an SQL Server database, file share, or web application. In a Silver Ticket attack, the attacker compromises the password hash of the service account associated with the target service's Service Principal Name. This is often done by dumping the memory of the service host or extracting keytab files.

Once the attacker has the service account's key, they can forge a service ticket offline without needing to communicate with the KDC. This forged ticket can then be used to authenticate directly to the target service, impersonating a legitimate user and bypassing the KDC entirely. Because Silver Ticket attacks bypass the Ticket Granting Service, they can be harder to detect than Golden Tickets, as there is no TGS request event generated in the Kerberos logs on the domain controller.

The scope of a Silver Ticket attack is more limited than a Golden Ticket, as it only grants access to the specific service tied to the compromised service account. However, in practice, this still provides significant risk. Attackers can use Silver Tickets to access databases, application servers, or file shares that contain sensitive data or are critical to business operations. In some cases, a Silver Ticket attack can serve as a stepping stone to further escalate privileges, especially if the targeted service has administrative access to other systems.

Mitigating the risks of Golden and Silver Ticket attacks starts with strong protection of privileged accounts and service principals. Since both attacks require access to sensitive keys, organizations must enforce strict access controls on domain controllers and service accounts. This includes using tiered administrative models to limit which users can log into domain controllers, regularly rotating krbtgt and service account passwords, and minimizing the number of accounts with elevated privileges.

Implementing security features such as Credential Guard can help mitigate memory dumping techniques used to extract krbtgt or service account hashes from compromised systems. Additionally, organizations should enforce modern encryption types for Kerberos, such as AES-256, to strengthen the cryptographic protection of tickets and session keys. Weak or deprecated encryption types like RC4 or DES should be disabled to reduce the risk of cryptographic attacks.

Monitoring and auditing Kerberos events are critical to detecting Golden and Silver Ticket attacks. Security teams should look for anomalies such as service tickets with unusually long lifetimes, tickets that include administrative privileges for unexpected accounts, or Kerberos tickets being used from non-standard systems. Golden Ticket usage may also manifest as tickets being presented from systems that do not normally authenticate to the domain, while Silver Ticket attacks may show up as service access occurring without a corresponding TGS request in the KDC logs.

Network segmentation and limiting the exposure of sensitive services can reduce the blast radius of a successful Silver Ticket attack. For instance, services that rely on Kerberos should be placed in separate network zones with tightly controlled access policies, ensuring that even if a service ticket is forged, the attacker cannot easily move laterally to other high-value targets.

Golden Ticket and Silver Ticket attacks have become core components of many advanced persistent threat campaigns and red team exercises because they exploit fundamental aspects of the Kerberos protocol's trust model. By targeting the mechanisms that validate ticket authenticity, attackers bypass many traditional security controls and can operate stealthily within compromised environments.

Organizations that rely on Kerberos must treat the protection of domain controllers, privileged accounts, and service principals as a top priority. The combination of preventive controls, continuous monitoring, and regular security assessments is necessary to safeguard against the destructive potential of Golden Ticket and Silver Ticket attacks.

# Defending Against Kerberos Attacks

Defending against Kerberos attacks requires a multifaceted approach that combines technical controls, policy enforcement, and continuous monitoring. While Kerberos is a secure authentication protocol when properly implemented, its complexity and integration with enterprise environments make it an attractive target for attackers. Threats such as Pass-the-Ticket, Pass-the-Hash, Golden Ticket, Silver Ticket, and Kerberoasting are just a few of the common attack techniques that exploit misconfigurations, poor credential management, and weak monitoring practices. To effectively defend against these attacks, organizations must adopt both preventive and detective security measures that harden their Kerberos environments.

One of the foundational defenses against Kerberos attacks is the protection of privileged accounts and domain controllers. Domain controllers, which function as Key Distribution Centers, must be treated as the most sensitive assets within the network. Only highly trusted and minimal personnel should be granted administrative access to domain controllers, and access should be performed from secure, hardened systems isolated from general workstation networks. Implementing tiered administrative models helps to separate administrative duties and prevents lower-level accounts from having unnecessary privileges over sensitive infrastructure. In addition, service accounts and the krbtgt account, whose keys are vital to the Kerberos trust model, must be protected with strong, randomly generated passwords and rotated regularly.

Preventing attacks like Golden Tickets starts with the security of the krbtgt account. The krbtgt account's password hash is used to sign all Ticket Granting Tickets within a Kerberos realm, and compromising this key allows attackers to forge TGTs with any level of privilege. Regular rotation of the krbtgt password, ideally every 180 days or more frequently depending on risk assessments, limits the window of opportunity for attackers. Password complexity and length are also critical; long, complex passwords significantly increase the difficulty of brute-forcing or cracking the krbtgt key in the event of a compromise.

Strong encryption settings further harden Kerberos environments. Organizations must disable deprecated encryption algorithms such as DES and RC4, which are vulnerable to cryptographic attacks, and enforce the use of modern encryption standards like AES-256. Ensuring that all Kerberos principals and services use these secure encryption types reduces the likelihood that attackers will exploit cryptographic weaknesses during ticket forgery or key brute-forcing attempts. Administrators should update Kerberos configuration files, Group Policy settings, and service principal attributes to mandate the use of strong encryption.

Kerberos delegation configurations must be reviewed and strictly controlled to prevent abuse. Unconstrained delegation allows services to impersonate users to any resource in the domain, significantly increasing the attack surface if such a service is compromised. To mitigate this risk, organizations should favor constrained delegation, where services are only permitted to delegate user credentials to specific backend services. An even more secure approach is resource-based constrained delegation, where the backend service defines which services are trusted to perform delegation. This granular control helps limit the lateral movement paths available to attackers using forged tickets or stolen credentials.

Endpoint security is another critical pillar of Kerberos defense. Many ticket-based attacks begin with compromising endpoint devices and extracting cached Kerberos tickets or password hashes from memory. Deploying solutions such as Microsoft's Credential Guard helps prevent attackers from dumping Kerberos tickets or NTLM hashes by isolating secrets in a secure virtualization-based environment. Hardening endpoints through regular patching, limiting local administrator accounts, and enforcing application whitelisting can significantly reduce the risk of credential theft.

Network segmentation and firewall policies play an important role in limiting lateral movement. By segmenting critical assets, such as domain controllers, databases, and application servers, into secure network zones, organizations make it more difficult for attackers to exploit stolen tickets or hashes across the network. Strict firewall rules should limit which systems can communicate with each other, forcing attackers to overcome additional barriers before reaching sensitive resources.

Monitoring and logging are indispensable components of defending against Kerberos attacks. Kerberos events should be forwarded to a centralized logging system, such as a Security Information and Event Management (SIEM) platform, where they can be correlated and analyzed for suspicious patterns. Indicators of compromise include Kerberos tickets being used from unusual endpoints, service tickets with excessively long lifetimes, or authentication attempts to services where no corresponding Ticket Granting Service request was logged. These anomalies often point to forged tickets or Pass-the-Ticket attacks.

Detecting Golden Ticket activity involves monitoring for unusual ticket usage from non-standard workstations or the appearance of high-privileged tickets on unexpected systems. Monitoring for Silver Ticket attacks requires paying attention to service logons that bypass the KDC, such as service ticket use without a corresponding TGS request. Additionally, the presence of service tickets with non-standard encryption types or suspicious timestamps may indicate a forgery attempt.

Auditing service principal configurations is also essential to prevent Kerberoasting attacks. Service accounts with weak passwords are prime targets because attackers can request and crack their service tickets offline. Enforcing complex and lengthy passwords for service accounts and removing unnecessary service principal names reduces the attack surface. For highly sensitive services, administrators can configure accounts to require smart card logon or disable Kerberos pre-authentication exemption flags that can be abused in AS-REP roasting attacks.

Security awareness and operational discipline must complement technical controls. Administrators and IT staff should receive regular training on Kerberos security best practices, including the risks associated with poor delegation configurations, improper SPN management, and the dangers of reusing privileged credentials across systems. Policies should require that privileged accounts are only used from dedicated jump boxes or administrative workstations and never for general web browsing or email activities, as these expose credentials to phishing and malware risks.

Finally, organizations should regularly conduct security assessments, such as penetration testing and red teaming exercises, to evaluate the effectiveness of their Kerberos defenses. Simulated attacks can help identify weak configurations, discover gaps in monitoring, and test incident response processes. Blue teams can use insights from these exercises to fine-tune detection rules, strengthen endpoint protection, and implement additional hardening measures to reduce risk.

By combining robust technical safeguards, well-defined administrative controls, and comprehensive monitoring, organizations can create a resilient defense against Kerberos-based attacks. Although Kerberos is a mature and secure protocol, its effectiveness is highly dependent on how well it is implemented and managed within enterprise networks. Proactive defense strategies help prevent credential abuse, detect intrusions early, and protect the integrity of critical authentication workflows that underpin secure access to systems and data.

# Logging and Monitoring Kerberos Events

Logging and monitoring Kerberos events are essential practices for maintaining the security and integrity of enterprise networks that rely on Kerberos for authentication. As Kerberos underpins the trust model for accessing critical resources such as file servers, databases, and applications, the ability to detect anomalies, unauthorized access attempts, and potential credential misuse is vital. Comprehensive logging provides valuable visibility into authentication workflows, while continuous monitoring enables organizations to respond swiftly to threats such as ticket forgery, lateral movement, and privilege escalation. By understanding the key events generated by Kerberos and configuring effective monitoring strategies, organizations can strengthen their defenses and improve their detection capabilities.

Kerberos generates various event logs that are essential for identifying suspicious activities. In Windows environments, these events are primarily logged within the Security log on domain controllers and client systems. Domain controllers serve as the Kerberos Key Distribution Centers and are responsible for issuing Ticket Granting Tickets and service tickets. As such, they are a critical source of Kerberos-related telemetry. Some of the most important Kerberos events include Ticket Granting Ticket requests (Event ID 4768), service ticket requests (Event ID 4769), and ticket renewal requests (Event ID 4770). Additionally, events such as failed ticket requests (Event ID 4771) or requests without pre-authentication (Event ID 4768 with a pre-authentication failure code) may indicate potential brute-force or password-spraying attacks.

Monitoring Event ID 4768 helps security teams track when a user successfully requests a Ticket Granting Ticket from the KDC. This event provides insight into who is authenticating, from which IP address or workstation, and at what time. By establishing baselines of normal login behavior, analysts can identify deviations, such as logins from unexpected locations or after business hours, that could suggest compromised credentials. Similarly, Event ID 4769 records service ticket requests to the Ticket Granting Service. Monitoring these events can reveal lateral movement attempts, particularly when accounts request tickets for services they do not typically access.

Failed Kerberos authentication attempts, logged under Event ID 4771, are especially important for detecting attacks against the Kerberos protocol. For instance, attackers may attempt Kerberoasting by requesting service tickets for service accounts and then attempting to crack them offline. A surge in Event ID 4771 entries targeting service accounts, particularly those with the RC4 encryption type, may indicate an active Kerberoasting campaign. Monitoring such patterns allows security teams to detect and respond to credential theft attempts before attackers gain access to sensitive accounts.

leading to lateral movement across domain-joined devices. In Windows environments, where NTLM is commonly used for local administrator accounts or legacy services, Pass-the-Hash can be particularly effective for expanding an attacker's footprint within the network.

Both attack techniques are frequently used as part of a broader strategy in Advanced Persistent Threat campaigns. Attackers often begin by compromising a low-privileged account or system and then leverage Pass-the-Ticket or Pass-the-Hash to escalate privileges and gain access to higher-value targets, such as domain controllers, file servers, or executive workstations. In cases where attackers obtain Kerberos tickets for privileged accounts or NTLM hashes for accounts with administrative rights, they can effectively control entire network segments.

A key enabler of both attack types is poor endpoint security hygiene. Systems with outdated software, weak configurations, or lax administrative controls are more susceptible to credential dumping. Additionally, shared accounts, local administrator accounts with identical passwords across multiple systems, and long-lived service accounts with static credentials provide attackers with multiple opportunities to harvest reusable authentication artifacts.

Defending against Pass-the-Ticket and Pass-the-Hash attacks requires a multi-layered approach. For Pass-the-Ticket, organizations must ensure that Kerberos tickets and credential caches are protected. Limiting the use of unconstrained delegation, enforcing short ticket lifetimes, and requiring mutual authentication between clients and services are essential defensive measures. Regularly clearing cached tickets when no longer needed, combined with session timeouts, can reduce the risk of stolen tickets being used for prolonged lateral movement.

For Pass-the-Hash mitigation, organizations should limit or eliminate the use of NTLM where possible, transitioning to Kerberos or other modern authentication protocols. Ensuring that each system has unique local administrator passwords, for example, through Local Administrator Password Solution (LAPS), helps reduce the impact of harvested hashes. Credential Guard, a security feature in Windows,

To maximize visibility, organizations should ensure that Kerberos auditing is enabled at both domain controller and client levels. On domain controllers, Kerberos service ticket operations, TGT requests, renewals, and failures should be logged, while on clients, ticket cache activity and authentication attempts to services are equally important. Additionally, enabling advanced auditing policies in Active Directory can capture more granular details, including ticket encryption types, logon process information, and the specific service principal name requested.

Organizations operating hybrid environments with cloud-integrated Active Directory should also ensure that Kerberos-related logs are forwarded to cloud-native monitoring platforms, such as Microsoft Sentinel or AWS Security Hub. Hybrid deployments introduce new attack vectors, as cloud-hosted resources may be targeted for credential theft or lateral movement. Integrating on-premises Kerberos telemetry with cloud-native monitoring ensures consistent visibility across both traditional and modern workloads.

Finally, regularly reviewing and tuning detection rules is critical to improving the effectiveness of Kerberos event monitoring. Threat actors continuously evolve their tactics, and organizations must adjust their detection mechanisms to account for new techniques. For example, detecting Silver Ticket attacks may involve analyzing service logon events (Event ID 4624) on targeted services and cross-referencing them with domain controller logs to verify if a corresponding service ticket request was ever made to the KDC. Absence of this request may indicate that a forged service ticket was used directly against the service, bypassing the domain controller.

Kerberos logging and monitoring serve as the first line of defense against a wide range of threats, from insider abuse to advanced persistent threats attempting to undermine authentication workflows. By leveraging the rich data available from Kerberos event logs and combining it with contextual information from other sources, security teams can gain deeper insight into the health and security of their identity infrastructure. Consistent vigilance, combined with automation and correlation through SIEM platforms, ensures that organizations can detect and respond to Kerberos-related attacks before significant damage occurs.

# Auditing Kerberos Deployments

Auditing Kerberos deployments is a crucial practice for maintaining the integrity, security, and efficiency of enterprise authentication infrastructures. Kerberos is the backbone of many organizations' identity management systems, particularly in environments where Active Directory or MIT Kerberos realms are used to secure access to critical resources. A thorough audit helps organizations identify misconfigurations, detect vulnerabilities, and ensure compliance with internal security policies and external regulations. The complexity and distributed nature of Kerberos environments demand a systematic and methodical approach to auditing every component of the deployment, from the Key Distribution Center to service principals, client configurations, ticket issuance policies, and delegation settings.

An effective audit begins with a comprehensive inventory of all Kerberos components within the environment. This includes identifying all domain controllers or Key Distribution Centers responsible for issuing and validating Kerberos tickets. In Active Directory-based environments, this typically involves auditing all domain controllers within the forest and ensuring that they are running supported versions of Windows Server, are fully patched, and are configured according to industry best practices. In MIT Kerberos environments, administrators must review the KDC infrastructure, ensuring redundancy and secure configurations.

Next, auditors should assess the Kerberos realm or domain settings, focusing on ticket lifetimes and renewal policies. These policies directly impact the window of opportunity attackers might have if they manage to compromise a Kerberos ticket. For instance, excessively long ticket lifetimes or unrestricted renewal periods can allow attackers to reuse stolen tickets for prolonged periods. Reviewing krbtgt account settings is also essential. Since the krbtgt account's key is used to sign all Ticket Granting Tickets, auditors must verify that its password is rotated regularly and that it is protected with a strong, complex password. Documentation should exist for the last password change, and plans should be in place for routine updates.

A critical aspect of auditing Kerberos deployments involves reviewing encryption policies. Auditors must ensure that deprecated encryption algorithms such as DES and RC4 are disabled across all accounts and that strong algorithms like AES-256 are enforced. This is typically managed via Group Policy Objects in Active Directory environments or through configuration files in MIT Kerberos setups. Weak encryption increases the risk of ticket forgery or offline password cracking attacks, making it a high-priority area for review.

Service Principal Name (SPN) management is another vital focus of Kerberos audits. SPNs uniquely identify services to the Kerberos realm, and misconfigurations or duplications can lead to authentication failures or create opportunities for exploitation, such as Service Principal Name spoofing. Auditors should compile an inventory of all SPNs registered in the environment, identify duplicates, and verify that each SPN is registered to the appropriate service account. It is also important to confirm that no critical SPNs are associated with user accounts unless explicitly necessary, as this may increase the risk of Kerberoasting attacks.

Auditing service accounts is closely tied to SPN management. Service accounts with associated SPNs are frequent targets for attackers seeking to perform offline password cracking or ticket forgery attacks. Auditors should ensure that all service accounts have complex, lengthy passwords and that password rotation policies are in place. Service accounts should also adhere to the principle of least privilege, meaning they should only have permissions necessary for their intended function. Where possible, service accounts should use managed service account options or be configured to require smart card authentication for additional security.

Delegation configurations within Kerberos deployments require particular attention. Improper use of unconstrained delegation can introduce serious security risks, as it allows services to impersonate users across the entire Kerberos realm. Auditors must review all delegation settings to verify that services only use constrained delegation or resource-based constrained delegation where necessary. In environments where unconstrained delegation is found, its justification should be carefully documented, and efforts should be made to migrate to more secure alternatives. Auditors should also ensure that delegation is not configured for high-privilege accounts, such as domain administrators, as this could be exploited for privilege escalation.

Time synchronization across all Kerberos clients, servers, and KDCs is critical to preventing authentication failures and replay attacks. Kerberos relies on timestamp verification, and clock skew beyond the accepted tolerance window—typically five minutes—can cause legitimate tickets to be rejected or exploited. Auditors should verify that all systems participate in a reliable time synchronization infrastructure, such as using NTP servers, and ensure that fallback configurations exist in case of time service disruptions.

Another essential component of a Kerberos audit is log review and monitoring assessment. Auditors must verify that Kerberos-related events are being properly logged on domain controllers, clients, and services. Critical events, including successful and failed ticket requests, ticket renewals, and authentication failures, should be forwarded to a centralized Security Information and Event Management system for correlation and analysis. Reviewing logs from a security perspective allows auditors to detect signs of credential abuse, such as Pass-the-Ticket or Kerberoasting attempts, and verify that incident response processes are in place to address detected anomalies.

In hybrid and cloud-integrated environments, auditors should also assess how Kerberos is integrated with identity federation and cloud authentication systems. This involves reviewing Azure AD Connect configurations, ensuring that synchronization settings are secure and that on-premises credentials are protected during federation with cloud identity providers. Hybrid environments often rely on additional services like Azure AD Application Proxy or custom security token services to bridge Kerberos authentication with cloud applications. Auditors must verify that these components are hardened and that they enforce secure communication protocols.

Auditing Kerberos deployments also includes examining endpoint configurations. Client systems should be configured to securely manage Kerberos credential caches, limit ticket exposure in memory, and prevent unauthorized access to sensitive Kerberos artifacts. Where applicable, security features like Microsoft Credential Guard should be enabled to protect against memory scraping attacks targeting Kerberos tickets or NTLM hashes.

Finally, auditors must ensure that administrative policies and documentation reflect Kerberos best practices. This includes documenting the password rotation schedule for krbtgt and service accounts, delegation and SPN assignments, encryption policies, and logging configurations. Regularly scheduled internal audits should be conducted to validate adherence to these policies, and any deviations should trigger corrective action.

Auditing Kerberos deployments is not a one-time task but an ongoing process that helps organizations adapt to evolving threats and maintain secure authentication workflows. By thoroughly reviewing the configuration and operation of Kerberos realms, organizations can proactively identify and address security gaps, ensure compliance with security frameworks, and strengthen the overall trust model that underpins access to critical enterprise resources.

# Troubleshooting Kerberos Authentication Failures

Troubleshooting Kerberos authentication failures is one of the more complex tasks facing system administrators, due to the intricate nature of the protocol and its reliance on multiple components working seamlessly together. Kerberos authentication relies on a series of steps that involve the client, the Key Distribution Center, the service, and the network infrastructure. A failure at any point in the process can result in an inability to access critical systems or services. To diagnose and resolve such failures, administrators must understand both the Kerberos protocol workflow and the most common sources of errors. A structured troubleshooting approach ensures that issues are identified quickly and that users and services can regain normal operation with minimal disruption.

One of the most common causes of Kerberos authentication failures is time synchronization discrepancies. Kerberos is a time-sensitive protocol that relies on synchronized clocks between clients, servers, and KDCs. If the clock skew exceeds the allowed threshold, typically set at five minutes, authentication attempts will fail due to ticket timestamps being outside of the valid window. Administrators should first verify that all systems are synchronized to a common and reliable time source, such as an internal or external NTP server. Tools like w32tm on Windows or ntpq on Linux can help validate time configurations and identify drift issues that may be causing authentication failures.

Service Principal Name misconfigurations are another frequent source of Kerberos errors. Each service that participates in Kerberos authentication must have a correctly registered SPN within the directory service or KDC database. Duplicate SPNs or missing SPNs will prevent the KDC from issuing valid service tickets, resulting in errors when clients attempt to access services. Administrators can use utilities like setspn on Windows to list and manage SPNs, checking for duplicates and verifying that the correct SPN is associated with the intended service account. For example, a web application running on host webserver01.example.com should have an SPN such as HTTP/webserver01.example.com@EXAMPLE.COM registered to its service account.

Incorrect keytab files or service account password changes are also common culprits of Kerberos failures. When a service account's password is changed, any keytab files that were previously generated for that service become invalid unless updated with the new credentials. A mismatch between the service ticket encryption and the service's keytab file will result in decryption failures, preventing the service from validating client tickets. Administrators should regenerate keytab files whenever service account credentials are updated and ensure that services are restarted to load the new keys.

DNS resolution issues often play a hidden but critical role in Kerberos authentication problems. Kerberos is heavily reliant on accurate DNS resolution to map hostnames to IP addresses and to match service principal names with fully qualified domain names. If clients resolve a service to an unexpected or incorrect hostname, the SPN presented in the ticket request may not match the expected service account, causing authentication to fail. Administrators should confirm that both forward and reverse DNS resolution are functioning correctly and that hostnames are registered properly in the DNS zone. In environments using Active Directory, verifying that dynamic DNS updates are working as intended is also essential.

Authentication failures may also stem from client-side misconfigurations, particularly in multi-realm or hybrid environments. For example, a client may attempt to request a ticket from an incorrect KDC if the Kerberos configuration file (krb5.conf on Linux or the registry settings on Windows) does not accurately map the realm to the correct KDC servers. Additionally, Kerberos clients may default to NTLM authentication if Kerberos configuration is incomplete or if fallback mechanisms are triggered due to ticket request failures. Administrators should inspect client configurations to ensure that they correctly point to the expected Kerberos realm and KDC servers, and that fallback to weaker protocols is disabled where possible.

Another common scenario involves issues related to delegation. Services configured for constrained delegation require specific settings that allow them to forward tickets on behalf of users to backend services. If delegation is misconfigured, services may fail when trying to act on behalf of users, leading to authentication errors. Administrators should review delegation settings in Active Directory, ensuring that the appropriate trust configurations and service principal mappings are in place. For resource-based constrained delegation, verification on both the intermediate and backend service accounts is necessary to confirm that delegation permissions are granted correctly.

Ticket expiration and caching issues can also contribute to intermittent Kerberos authentication problems. Clients cache both TGTs and service tickets, and if a cached ticket expires or is corrupted, authentication failures may occur until the ticket is refreshed. Clearing the Kerberos ticket cache using kdestroy on Linux or klist purge on Windows forces the client to request fresh tickets from the KDC. Additionally, administrators should verify that ticket lifetimes and renewal policies are appropriate for their environment, balancing security and usability.

Kerberos pre-authentication failures can indicate password mismatch issues or brute-force attack attempts. When reviewing logs, an event such as Event ID 4771 on Windows with a Kerberos pre-authentication failure code can point administrators to users entering incorrect passwords or to potential malicious activity. Administrators should validate that account credentials are correct and, where necessary, investigate further to determine if a broader security incident is underway.

In troubleshooting scenarios, reviewing logs is indispensable. Kerberos-related events generated on domain controllers, services, and clients offer invaluable insight into the failure points of authentication processes. Event logs such as 4768 (TGT requests), 4769 (TGS requests), and 4771 (pre-authentication failures) can help identify where in the Kerberos flow the problem is occurring. Capturing Kerberos traffic using tools like Wireshark allows administrators to observe ticket exchanges, inspect SPNs in ticket requests, and diagnose encryption mismatches or KDC referral loops.

Finally, addressing Kerberos authentication failures often requires cross-functional collaboration between infrastructure teams, application owners, and security personnel. Complex failures may involve network issues, application-level misconfigurations, or Active Directory schema limitations. By following a methodical approach that includes validating time synchronization, inspecting DNS configurations, reviewing SPNs and keytab files, analyzing logs, and confirming client configurations, administrators can systematically resolve Kerberos authentication issues and restore normal operations to the environment. Troubleshooting Kerberos is a process that benefits from both deep technical understanding and attention to detail across all layers of the authentication ecosystem.

# Kerberos Performance Optimization

Kerberos performance optimization is an essential consideration for organizations that depend on Kerberos for secure authentication across enterprise networks. While Kerberos is a highly efficient protocol, capable of providing rapid and secure authentication, poor configurations, hardware limitations, and network latency can introduce delays and inefficiencies that degrade the user experience and impact the performance of services that rely on Kerberos. Optimizing Kerberos not only improves authentication speeds but also enhances the stability and scalability of the entire authentication infrastructure. A well-tuned Kerberos environment minimizes authentication-related bottlenecks and ensures that the protocol delivers on its promise of fast, secure, and seamless identity verification.

One of the first areas to examine when optimizing Kerberos performance is the placement and configuration of the Key Distribution Center, which is a critical component responsible for processing Ticket Granting Ticket and service ticket requests. In larger environments, deploying multiple KDCs or domain controllers across geographically distributed sites helps reduce latency by bringing authentication services closer to clients. Organizations should ensure that their KDCs are load-balanced to prevent any single instance from becoming a bottleneck. In Active Directory environments, sites and services should be configured to ensure clients authenticate against local domain controllers rather than remote ones, reducing the time needed to acquire tickets and preventing unnecessary WAN traffic.

The performance of Kerberos is also influenced by the underlying network infrastructure. Latency between clients and KDCs can significantly impact ticket request and renewal times. To address this, administrators should evaluate the network paths between clients and their designated KDCs, ensuring that routing is optimized and that firewall policies do not introduce unnecessary inspection or delay for Kerberos traffic. Kerberos relies on UDP and TCP port 88 for ticket exchanges and port 464 for password changes, so these ports must be prioritized and monitored for packet loss or excessive jitter.

Another critical factor in optimizing Kerberos performance is ticket lifetime and renewal settings. While longer ticket lifetimes reduce the frequency of ticket renewals, they may also increase the risk of ticket misuse if a ticket is compromised. Conversely, overly short ticket lifetimes can flood the KDC with excessive ticket requests, increasing the load on domain controllers and slowing down authentication processes. Administrators should carefully tune the maximum ticket lifetime, maximum renewal lifetime, and service ticket expiration settings to strike a balance between performance and security.

Common best practices suggest ticket lifetimes between 8 and 10 hours, with renewal periods set to one week, but these values may vary depending on organizational needs.

Kerberos pre-authentication, while an essential security feature, can also introduce additional overhead in high-frequency authentication scenarios. Pre-authentication requires clients to submit an encrypted timestamp during the initial ticket request, adding computational load on both the client and the KDC. In certain controlled environments, pre-authentication may be selectively disabled for specific service accounts to reduce this overhead, although this must be weighed carefully against security considerations, as disabling pre-authentication can expose accounts to offline password-guessing attacks.

Improving Kerberos cache management on clients is another opportunity for performance optimization. Kerberos clients maintain a ticket cache that stores active Ticket Granting Tickets and service tickets to avoid repeated requests to the KDC for frequently accessed services. Administrators should ensure that client-side ticket caches are configured properly and that policies support appropriate ticket reuse. On Windows systems, Group Policy Objects can control ticket cache behavior, while on Linux systems using MIT Kerberos, settings in krb5.conf determine cache management. Efficient ticket caching minimizes repeated network round trips and reduces KDC load, improving responsiveness for users accessing multiple services in rapid succession.

Service Principal Name configuration is also important for performance. A missing or improperly registered SPN can cause authentication requests to fail and fall back to slower methods such as NTLM, degrading performance. Administrators should audit SPNs regularly to ensure that all services participating in Kerberos authentication have correct and unique SPN entries in the directory. Additionally, SPN delegation chains should be minimized, as lengthy delegation configurations can result in additional ticket exchanges and delays in establishing secure sessions between clients and services.

Optimizing Kerberos encryption settings is equally important. Modern Kerberos implementations support multiple encryption algorithms, with AES-256 generally considered the most secure and efficient for most environments. Using strong encryption algorithms not only enhances security but can also improve performance when compared to legacy algorithms like DES, which may not be hardware-accelerated on modern processors. Organizations should ensure that clients and servers support hardware-accelerated cryptographic operations, as this can reduce the CPU load associated with ticket encryption and decryption, especially in high-traffic environments.

On the client side, administrators should ensure that Kerberos libraries and software are up to date. Updates often include performance enhancements, improved caching mechanisms, and bug fixes that can resolve hidden inefficiencies in the authentication process. Modern Kerberos clients may also include optimizations such as improved ticket renewal logic, reducing unnecessary KDC traffic. Clients should be configured to leverage DNS lookups efficiently, using short and fully qualified domain names to minimize resolution delays that may impact SPN matching and ticket requests.

Monitoring KDC performance is another key practice in optimization. Administrators should track metrics such as the number of ticket requests per second, ticket renewal rates, and CPU and memory usage on KDC servers. Sudden spikes in ticket request volume could indicate misconfigurations, application issues, or security incidents such as brute-force attacks. Proactive capacity planning, such as provisioning additional KDCs in busy regions or increasing server resources, helps ensure that authentication workloads are handled smoothly under varying conditions.

In hybrid environments, where on-premises Kerberos realms integrate with cloud services, administrators must also consider the impact of federation and proxy services on authentication performance. When cloud-based applications rely on Kerberos tickets issued by on-premises KDCs, the network path between the cloud and the data center becomes a critical performance factor. Using dedicated private links such as Azure ExpressRoute or AWS Direct Connect can help minimize latency and improve reliability for cloud-integrated Kerberos authentication workflows.

Finally, continuous review and refinement of Kerberos policies ensure that the environment evolves alongside changes in user behavior, application workloads, and network topology. As new services are added or usage patterns shift, administrators should revisit Kerberos configurations to fine-tune ticket lifetimes, cache settings, and KDC placement to maintain optimal performance. By systematically addressing these various dimensions of Kerberos optimization, organizations can achieve a high-performing, secure, and scalable authentication infrastructure that meets the demands of modern enterprise environments.

# Upgrading and Migrating Kerberos Systems

Upgrading and migrating Kerberos systems is a critical task that requires careful planning, precise execution, and a thorough understanding of both the existing and target environments. Kerberos serves as the backbone of authentication in many enterprise networks, and any disruption to its operation can have widespread impacts on user access, service availability, and security posture. Whether upgrading an existing Kerberos realm to a newer version or migrating from one Kerberos implementation to another, organizations must address several technical and operational considerations to ensure a smooth transition while preserving security, functionality, and performance.

The first step in any Kerberos upgrade or migration project is to perform a comprehensive assessment of the current environment. This includes documenting the existing Key Distribution Center infrastructure, service principal names, realm configurations, and integration points with applications and services. Administrators should inventory all Kerberos clients and servers, determine the versions of the Kerberos software in use, and identify any custom configurations or non-standard deployments. For example, some organizations may use MIT Kerberos for Linux-based systems and integrate it with Microsoft Active Directory for cross-platform authentication, necessitating a hybrid approach to the upgrade or migration process.

One of the primary reasons for upgrading Kerberos systems is to take advantage of enhanced security features, performance improvements, and support for modern encryption algorithms. Older versions of Kerberos may rely on deprecated encryption types such as DES or RC4, which are vulnerable to cryptographic attacks. Upgrading to a newer Kerberos version enables organizations to enforce the use of AES-256 or other secure ciphers, reducing the risk of ticket forgery or brute-force attacks. During the upgrade, administrators must carefully review and adjust encryption policies across the realm to ensure compatibility with all services and clients.

In-place upgrades are a common approach when updating to newer Kerberos software versions within the same realm. For example, upgrading from an older version of MIT Kerberos to a more recent release typically involves installing updated packages, applying configuration changes, and restarting services on the KDC and clients. Prior to performing the upgrade, administrators should create comprehensive system backups, including the KDC database, keytab files, and configuration files such as krb5.conf. Testing the upgrade in a lab environment or a non-production realm is highly recommended to identify and resolve potential issues before deployment to the production environment.

When migrating Kerberos systems, such as moving from an MIT Kerberos deployment to a Microsoft Active Directory-based Kerberos realm, the complexity increases. Migration projects often require setting up a parallel Kerberos infrastructure alongside the existing environment and gradually transitioning services and clients. Cross-realm trust relationships can be established to enable coexistence between the source and target realms, allowing users and services in one realm to authenticate to resources in the other. This phased approach minimizes downtime and ensures that authentication continuity is maintained throughout the migration process.

Migrating service principals is a critical component of the transition. Each service that relies on Kerberos must have its Service Principal Name registered in the target realm, and the corresponding keytab files must be regenerated using keys derived from the target KDC. Administrators should audit existing SPNs to ensure there are no duplicates or conflicts that could cause authentication issues after migration. During this process, care must be taken to synchronize DNS records and verify that client machines resolve hostnames correctly to avoid SPN mismatches.

Client reconfiguration is another key step in the migration process. Kerberos clients need updated krb5.conf files or equivalent settings to recognize and trust the target KDC servers and realms. On Linux and Unix systems using MIT Kerberos or Heimdal, this often involves updating the realm and KDC sections of the configuration file. In Active Directory environments, Group Policy settings can be used to direct Windows clients to the appropriate domain controllers acting as KDCs. Any services relying on Kerberos, such as web servers, databases, and file servers, must also be reconfigured to accept tickets from the new realm.

Security hardening should accompany any Kerberos upgrade or migration. This includes enforcing strong ticket policies, such as limiting ticket lifetimes, enabling pre-authentication, and configuring delegation settings to minimize attack surfaces. Additionally, new features available in upgraded Kerberos versions, such as FAST (Flexible Authentication Secure Tunneling), should be evaluated and implemented where appropriate to further enhance protection against credential-based attacks.

Testing is crucial during both upgrades and migrations. Administrators should validate that clients can successfully request and use Ticket Granting Tickets and service tickets from the target KDC. Service-to-service authentication flows should be thoroughly tested, especially for applications that depend on constrained or resource-based constrained delegation. Log files from both clients and KDCs should be reviewed for errors or anomalies, and performance metrics should be collected to compare pre- and post-migration authentication latencies.

Communication and change management play an important role in the success of Kerberos transitions. Users should be informed of any changes that may affect their login experience or access to networked services, especially if client-side reconfiguration or new credential issuance is required. Change control processes should include rollback plans in case of unforeseen issues during or after the transition.

Finally, once the upgrade or migration is completed, administrators should monitor the environment closely to identify and resolve any lingering authentication issues. Integrating the upgraded Kerberos infrastructure with Security Information and Event Management platforms ensures that suspicious activity is detected promptly, while ongoing audits and health checks validate the long-term success of the project.

Upgrading and migrating Kerberos systems is a technically demanding but rewarding initiative that strengthens the security and performance of enterprise authentication workflows. By following a systematic process that includes assessment, planning, testing, and post-deployment validation, organizations can successfully modernize their Kerberos infrastructure and align it with contemporary security and operational best practices.

# Kerberos and PKI Integration

Kerberos and Public Key Infrastructure integration provides a robust security framework by combining the benefits of symmetric key cryptography with the scalability and flexibility of digital certificates. Traditionally, Kerberos has been based on the use of shared secret keys for both client and service authentication. While highly efficient, this model has limitations, especially in environments where managing large numbers of keys and identities can become operationally complex. Integrating PKI into Kerberos addresses these challenges by allowing authentication workflows to incorporate digital certificates, enhancing security, simplifying key management, and supporting additional use cases such as smart card logon and secure communications across organizational boundaries.

One of the most common implementations of Kerberos and PKI integration is the use of Public Key Cryptography for Initial Authentication in Kerberos, commonly referred to as PKINIT. PKINIT extends the standard Kerberos protocol by enabling clients to use X.509 certificates instead of passwords when requesting an initial Ticket Granting Ticket from the Key Distribution Center. In this model, clients present their digital certificate and prove possession of the corresponding private key during the Authentication Service exchange, establishing a secure session without relying on shared secrets. This approach aligns with enterprise security policies that favor certificate-based authentication and supports strong, multi-factor authentication mechanisms such as smart cards.

Integrating PKI with Kerberos via PKINIT significantly enhances security by mitigating risks associated with password-based authentication. Passwords, even when combined with pre-authentication mechanisms, are susceptible to brute-force, phishing, and credential theft attacks. By replacing or augmenting passwords with certificates protected by hardware devices like smart cards or USB tokens, organizations can enforce higher assurance levels and meet regulatory compliance requirements. PKINIT also introduces Perfect Forward Secrecy, as session keys are negotiated using ephemeral Diffie-Hellman keys, ensuring that compromising long-term keys does not retroactively expose past session data.

The process of integrating PKI with Kerberos typically starts with the deployment of a trusted certificate authority that issues certificates to users and systems. The Key Distribution Center must also possess a valid certificate signed by a CA that is trusted by the clients. The KDC certificate is used to establish a mutual trust relationship with clients during the PKINIT exchange. Both the KDC and the clients perform certificate validation, ensuring that certificates are properly signed, have not expired, and are not listed on a Certificate Revocation List or invalidated through Online Certificate Status Protocol checks.

Kerberos environments that integrate with PKI often use smart card logon as a common authentication method. In this scenario, users insert their smart card into a reader, and the operating system initiates the Kerberos PKINIT process using the certificate and private key stored on the smart card. The result is a seamless Single Sign-On experience where the user authenticates once and obtains a Ticket Granting Ticket, which is then used to access services throughout the network without further credential prompts. Smart card logon is widely adopted in government, military, and financial sectors, where strict identity verification standards are enforced.

PKI integration also simplifies cross-realm authentication and federation. In environments with multiple Kerberos realms that must interoperate securely, PKI facilitates the establishment of trust relationships between realms without relying solely on shared keys. By issuing certificates to KDCs in each realm and configuring cross-realm PKINIT support, organizations can create secure authentication bridges, allowing users from one realm to access services in another using certificate-based trust. This is particularly valuable in large federated environments or mergers and acquisitions, where unifying identity infrastructure may take time.

From a technical perspective, enabling PKINIT requires modifying Kerberos configuration files to specify the relevant PKI parameters. In MIT Kerberos, administrators must configure krb5.conf to point to the PKINIT anchor certificate file, define the PKINIT identity for the client, and specify supported encryption types. The KDC's kdc.conf file must also be updated to include the KDC certificate and private key, and to enforce PKINIT requirements for specific client principals or globally across the realm. Similarly, Active Directory-based Kerberos implementations automatically support PKINIT when integrated with Windows Certificate Services and Group Policy configurations for smart card logon.

While PKI enhances Kerberos authentication, it introduces additional considerations related to certificate lifecycle management. Certificates must be issued, distributed, renewed, and revoked according to organizational policies. Automation tools, such as enterprise certificate management platforms, can streamline these tasks by integrating with directory services and Kerberos infrastructure to ensure certificates remain valid and are rotated before expiration. Failure to properly manage certificates can lead to authentication outages if expired or revoked certificates are used during the PKINIT process.

Performance is another consideration when integrating PKI with Kerberos. The PKINIT process introduces additional computational overhead compared to traditional Kerberos exchanges, as it requires public key operations, certificate validation, and Diffie-Hellman key exchanges. Organizations deploying PKINIT at scale should evaluate the performance capabilities of their KDC infrastructure and consider deploying hardware security modules or cryptographic accelerators if necessary to offload intensive cryptographic operations.

PKI integration also enhances Kerberos' ability to support secure communications at the service level. For example, services that rely on Kerberos tickets for authentication can also leverage TLS certificates for data encryption and integrity protection during session establishment. By combining Kerberos and PKI, organizations can implement layered security models where Kerberos secures identity verification and TLS ensures that the data exchanged between clients and services remains encrypted and tamper-proof.

Logging and auditing play a crucial role in Kerberos and PKI integration. The introduction of PKINIT generates specific events in KDC logs and client event logs, which can be monitored for compliance and security purposes. Logs should capture certificate usage, validation outcomes, and authentication success or failure events. Organizations must ensure that SIEM platforms are configured to detect anomalies related to certificate-based authentication, such as repeated PKINIT failures, use of revoked certificates, or authentication attempts from unauthorized clients.

In modern enterprise environments, integrating Kerberos with PKI provides a forward-looking approach to securing authentication processes, improving trust models, and aligning with industry security frameworks such as NIST SP 800-63. By combining the proven strengths of Kerberos with the flexibility and cryptographic assurances of PKI, organizations can build a resilient authentication infrastructure capable of supporting diverse use cases, including multi-factor authentication, secure federation, and highly sensitive workloads that demand the highest levels of identity assurance. The successful deployment of Kerberos and PKI integration ultimately strengthens the foundation of enterprise security and enables organizations to meet evolving operational and regulatory demands.

# Kerberos in Zero Trust Architectures

Kerberos, traditionally designed to secure authentication within trusted enterprise networks, has taken on a new and evolving role as organizations move toward Zero Trust architectures. Zero Trust shifts the security model from implicit trust based on network location to explicit verification of every user, device, and service attempting to access enterprise resources. In this context, Kerberos continues to serve as a foundational identity and authentication technology, but its integration within Zero Trust frameworks requires rethinking how it is deployed, monitored, and augmented to align with modern security principles.

In classic Kerberos deployments, authentication workflows assume that entities within the internal network are inherently trusted once authenticated. Users log into their domain-joined devices, receive a Ticket Granting Ticket from the Key Distribution Center, and use service tickets to access applications, databases, and other internal services. However, Zero Trust explicitly rejects this perimeter-based model, asserting that no entity should be trusted by default, even when operating inside the network. To adapt Kerberos to Zero Trust environments, organizations must pair Kerberos authentication with continuous verification mechanisms that evaluate trust signals dynamically, ensuring that access decisions are enforced not just at the initial login but throughout the session lifecycle.

One key adaptation is the integration of Kerberos with strong identity governance and device posture assessment. In a Zero Trust framework, Kerberos authentication alone is not sufficient to grant resource access. Instead, authentication workflows must be supplemented with contextual signals, such as device compliance status, geographic location, time of day, and user risk profile. Solutions such as Conditional Access policies and Endpoint Detection and Response agents feed this information into access control decisions, ensuring that Kerberos tickets are only honored when the requesting device and user meet defined security criteria. This integration is especially important for mitigating credential theft scenarios, where valid Kerberos tickets may be extracted from a compromised endpoint and replayed to access other resources.

The use of short-lived tickets and dynamic reauthentication is another strategy for aligning Kerberos with Zero Trust. Traditional Kerberos deployments often issue tickets valid for eight to ten hours, or longer if renewable. While convenient, this practice conflicts with the Zero Trust principle of minimizing implicit trust. By reducing ticket lifetimes and requiring reauthentication based on real-time risk assessments, organizations can limit the window of opportunity for attackers to exploit stolen tickets. Modern Kerberos implementations allow administrators to define granular ticket policies and leverage technologies such as FAST (Flexible Authentication Secure Tunneling) to strengthen ticket issuance and renewal processes.

Another important consideration is segmentation and micro-segmentation. In Zero Trust networks, lateral movement between systems is heavily restricted, and access to resources is granted on a least-privilege basis. Kerberos fits into this model by continuing to provide secure authentication between clients and services; however, network segmentation and strict firewall rules prevent clients from freely communicating with all KDCs or services within the environment. Instead, organizations can design Kerberos realms and trust relationships to align with segmented network zones, ensuring that tickets are only valid within specific segments and that cross-segment access requires additional verification or approval.

Kerberos' support for mutual authentication plays a critical role in Zero Trust, where validating the identity of services is just as important as authenticating users. When a client presents a service ticket to a resource, Kerberos enables both the client and service to verify each other's identities, reducing the risk of rogue services impersonating legitimate applications. Mutual authentication, enforced consistently across the network, strengthens defenses against man-in-the-middle attacks, a key threat in environments where implicit trust is eliminated.

Zero Trust architectures also require heightened monitoring and visibility into Kerberos activity. Organizations must deploy centralized logging and real-time analytics to track ticket issuance, service ticket usage, and unusual authentication patterns. Security teams should correlate Kerberos logs with endpoint and network telemetry to detect suspicious activity, such as Pass-the-Ticket attacks, lateral movement using stolen tickets, or anomalous ticket requests from non-standard locations. Integrating Kerberos event data into Security Information and Event Management platforms enhances threat detection and supports automated incident response workflows, essential components of a Zero Trust strategy.

Privileged Access Management is another layer where Kerberos operates within a Zero Trust framework. High-privilege accounts, such as domain administrators, should never be granted unrestricted or long-term access to sensitive systems. Instead, just-in-time access models can be implemented, where Kerberos tickets for privileged roles are only issued following a workflow that includes multi-factor authentication, managerial approval, or compliance verification. This approach ensures that even privileged users must pass continuous trust validation before obtaining access to critical resources, limiting exposure in the event of credential compromise.

Kerberos is also frequently integrated with identity federation systems in Zero Trust environments, particularly in hybrid and cloud scenarios. By federating on-premises Kerberos realms with cloud identity providers, organizations can extend Zero Trust policies to both internal and cloud-hosted applications. For example, a user might authenticate to the on-premises Kerberos realm and obtain a Ticket Granting Ticket, but before accessing a cloud application, the identity federation system applies additional controls such as device compliance checks, behavioral analytics, or geo-fencing rules. The combined use of Kerberos authentication and cloud-based conditional access ensures that identity assertions from Kerberos are only trusted when they meet modern Zero Trust requirements.

Additionally, organizations can extend Zero Trust principles to Kerberos delegation scenarios. Delegation allows services to act on behalf of users when accessing downstream services, a powerful but potentially risky feature. In Zero Trust environments, organizations should enforce resource-based constrained delegation, limiting which services can delegate credentials and specifying exactly which backend services can be accessed through delegation. This reduces the attack surface for lateral movement and limits the potential for misuse of delegation in multi-tier application architectures.

Lastly, user awareness and security culture are crucial to the success of Kerberos in Zero Trust implementations. While technical controls can enforce least-privilege access and continuous authentication, users must be trained to recognize security risks associated with credential theft, phishing, and unauthorized access attempts. By combining Kerberos with Zero Trust policies, security teams can ensure that authentication workflows are supported by human factors that reinforce vigilance and adherence to best practices.

Kerberos continues to be a vital component of modern security architectures, and when integrated with Zero Trust principles, it enhances both identity security and operational flexibility. By adopting a holistic approach that includes network segmentation, dynamic trust evaluation, continuous monitoring, and tightly controlled delegation, organizations can successfully adapt Kerberos to support Zero Trust initiatives. In doing so, they strengthen their defenses against modern threats and ensure that their authentication infrastructure remains resilient, secure, and aligned with the evolving demands of the digital enterprise.

# Emerging Trends in Kerberos Security

Kerberos has been a cornerstone of enterprise security for decades, providing a trusted and scalable method for authenticating users and services in distributed systems. However, as cyber threats become increasingly sophisticated and enterprise environments evolve, new trends are shaping how Kerberos is implemented and secured. These trends are driven by a combination of technological advancements, the rise of hybrid cloud architectures, and the adoption of modern security frameworks such as Zero Trust. Staying ahead of these developments is crucial for organizations seeking to strengthen their defenses against credential-based attacks while ensuring that Kerberos remains a reliable component of their security posture.

One major trend in Kerberos security is the increasing emphasis on modern cryptographic standards and the phasing out of legacy encryption protocols. Historically, Kerberos supported weaker algorithms such as DES and RC4, which have since been proven vulnerable to various cryptanalytic attacks. Today, organizations are accelerating the adoption of AES-256 encryption for Kerberos tickets and session keys. AES-256 not only provides stronger protection against brute-force and dictionary attacks but also aligns with regulatory frameworks like NIST guidelines and GDPR that mandate the use of modern cryptography. Future iterations of Kerberos are expected to incorporate even stronger encryption methods and cryptographic agility, allowing enterprises to adapt more quickly to emerging standards.

Another significant development is the integration of Kerberos with multi-factor authentication solutions. Traditionally, Kerberos has relied on a single-factor model where users authenticate using a password to request a Ticket Granting Ticket. As attackers have become adept at stealing or guessing credentials, organizations are increasingly augmenting Kerberos with smart card logins, biometric authentication, or hardware tokens. The use of PKINIT (Public Key Cryptography for Initial Authentication in Kerberos) is growing in popularity, allowing users to authenticate with X.509 certificates and private keys instead of passwords. This trend reduces reliance on shared secrets, strengthens identity assurance, and mitigates the risks of phishing and password spraying attacks.

Kerberos is also adapting to cloud-native environments, where traditional perimeter-based security models are being replaced by flexible, distributed architectures. In hybrid environments, where on-premises Kerberos realms coexist with cloud-based identity providers, there is a growing trend of federating Kerberos authentication with cloud services. Solutions such as Azure AD Connect enable organizations to bridge their on-premises Active Directory-based Kerberos realms with Azure Active Directory, supporting seamless Single Sign-On across on-premises and cloud-hosted applications. As more workloads move to the cloud, Kerberos will continue to evolve to support hybrid identity models, enabling secure cross-boundary authentication while complying with modern access policies.

Zero Trust security frameworks are shaping another emerging trend in Kerberos usage. Zero Trust dictates that no device, user, or service is trusted by default, even inside the traditional enterprise perimeter. In this context, Kerberos must now operate within environments where continuous authentication, real-time risk assessments, and least-privilege access policies are mandatory. Organizations are reconfiguring Kerberos realms to issue short-lived tickets, integrate with conditional access platforms, and enforce micro-segmentation. Kerberos' role in providing mutual authentication and secure ticket exchanges fits naturally within Zero Trust models, but its deployment must now be tightly coupled with monitoring and analytics platforms to detect anomalies and prevent credential misuse.

Machine learning and artificial intelligence are being increasingly applied to enhance Kerberos security monitoring and incident response. Traditional Kerberos logs provide valuable information about ticket issuance, renewals, and service access, but the sheer volume of data can overwhelm human analysts. Emerging security platforms are leveraging AI to identify patterns and anomalies in Kerberos authentication workflows, such as unusual ticket lifetimes, atypical service ticket usage, or lateral movement attempts indicative of Pass-the-Ticket or Golden Ticket attacks. AI-driven insights enable security teams to respond more rapidly to threats and reduce the risk of credential-based breaches going undetected.

The rise of containerization and microservices is also influencing how Kerberos is deployed and secured. In modern DevOps environments, applications are often deployed as containers across Kubernetes clusters or other orchestration platforms. These workloads frequently need to access legacy Kerberos-protected services, such as databases or file shares. As a result, organizations are adapting Kerberos configurations to support secure ticket handling within dynamic, containerized environments. This includes the automation of keytab file distribution, implementing secure ticket caches within ephemeral containers, and using service accounts with limited privileges. Additionally, cloud-native security tools are being developed to enable Kerberos authentication workflows that are compatible with the scalability and automation requirements of microservices architectures.

Another emerging trend is the expansion of Kerberos support into non-traditional platforms. Historically tied to enterprise environments, Kerberos is increasingly being adapted for use in emerging technologies, including edge computing and Internet of Things (IoT) devices. While these devices often operate in resource-constrained environments, there is growing interest in leveraging Kerberos' ticket-based model to secure communication between devices and centralized services. Lightweight Kerberos clients and specialized authentication gateways are being explored to extend Kerberos authentication into environments that traditionally relied on less secure methods.

Privacy-preserving enhancements are also influencing Kerberos developments. Researchers and security practitioners are exploring mechanisms to limit the exposure of user identities and sensitive metadata during ticket exchanges. Techniques such as anonymous Kerberos, where client identities are obscured until mutual trust is established, are being considered in privacy-sensitive environments. These advancements are particularly relevant for organizations that must comply with strict data protection regulations while maintaining strong authentication workflows.

Finally, the integration of Kerberos with emerging identity standards such as OAuth 2.0 and OpenID Connect is gaining momentum. While Kerberos excels at securing internal enterprise resources, modern web applications and APIs often rely on token-based authentication models. To bridge this gap, federated solutions are being developed that convert Kerberos tickets into OAuth or SAML tokens, enabling seamless interoperability between Kerberos-protected environments and modern web-based applications. This trend enhances the usability of Kerberos in heterogeneous ecosystems, allowing organizations to maintain consistent security models across legacy and cloud-native applications.

As cyber threats continue to evolve, the security community's focus on Kerberos will intensify, driving innovations that improve its resilience, scalability, and adaptability. The intersection of Kerberos with Zero Trust, AI-driven threat detection, and cloud-native architectures reflects the protocol's ongoing evolution from a legacy authentication system to a modern security cornerstone capable of meeting the demands of today's complex IT environments. Organizations that stay informed about these emerging trends will be better positioned to strengthen their Kerberos deployments, mitigate credential-related threats, and ensure that their authentication infrastructure remains robust and future-proof.

# Comparing Kerberos with Modern Alternatives

Kerberos has long been regarded as a foundational protocol for securing authentication in enterprise networks, particularly in environments such as Active Directory. Its ticket-based, symmetric key model and mutual authentication capabilities have provided a reliable and secure framework for decades. However, as IT infrastructures have evolved toward cloud-native services, distributed applications, and decentralized workforces, modern alternatives to Kerberos have gained prominence. Protocols and frameworks such as OAuth 2.0, OpenID Connect, and SAML have emerged to address new requirements, including user-centric web applications, federated identity, and cross-organizational trust. Comparing Kerberos to these modern alternatives reveals distinct strengths and limitations that influence their adoption based on organizational needs, deployment models, and security priorities.

Kerberos is a network authentication protocol designed to operate within a closed and trusted environment. It was originally developed for MIT's Project Athena and became widely adopted in Windows-based domains. Kerberos relies on symmetric key cryptography and a centralized Key Distribution Center that issues time-sensitive tickets to clients and services. This enables mutual authentication while protecting against common threats such as credential replay attacks. Kerberos is highly efficient in environments with domain-joined devices and services where the KDC and the clients share the same trusted infrastructure. The Single Sign-On capability provided by Kerberos ensures that users authenticate once and can access multiple internal services without repeatedly entering credentials.

In contrast, OAuth 2.0 is an authorization framework primarily designed to provide secure delegated access to web applications and APIs. Unlike Kerberos, OAuth 2.0 does not authenticate users directly but instead issues access tokens to third-party applications after users grant them consent. OAuth 2.0 is based on token exchanges and bearer tokens, which can be passed between web clients, APIs, and resource servers. It is particularly suited for modern cloud-native applications, mobile platforms, and Software as a Service offerings, where users and applications often operate outside the boundaries of a single trusted network. OAuth's stateless and flexible architecture makes it ideal for dynamic, internet-facing environments, though it lacks built-in mutual authentication or encryption, relying instead on underlying transport security such as TLS.

OpenID Connect is a modern identity layer built on top of OAuth 2.0. It introduces the concept of identity tokens, allowing OAuth to handle both authorization and user authentication in web-based applications. OpenID Connect supports federated identity, enabling users to authenticate using an external identity provider such as Google, Microsoft, or Okta. This is a departure from Kerberos' model, where authentication occurs within a single realm or through explicit cross-realm trust. OpenID Connect is widely adopted for public web services, consumer applications, and multi-tenant cloud services where users from various organizations or domains need seamless access to shared resources.

SAML (Security Assertion Markup Language) is another protocol commonly compared with Kerberos. SAML is an XML-based framework designed for federated identity and Single Sign-On across organizational boundaries. It enables identity providers to issue signed authentication assertions to service providers, allowing users to log in once and gain access to multiple external services. SAML is frequently used in business-to-business and enterprise SaaS contexts, where it supports cross-domain authentication through web browsers. Compared to Kerberos, SAML operates primarily over HTTP using browser redirects and POST messages, making it more suitable for web applications but less efficient for securing non-HTTP services such as file shares, database connections, or legacy applications.

A key difference between Kerberos and its modern alternatives is the trust model. Kerberos operates within a closed system where the KDC, clients, and services all belong to the same realm or have explicitly configured trust relationships. This makes Kerberos highly efficient in securing internal environments but limits its ability to scale seamlessly to external domains or cloud platforms. OAuth, OpenID Connect, and SAML, on the other hand, are designed for federated identity scenarios where multiple organizations or external identity providers collaborate without sharing a centralized authentication infrastructure. These protocols simplify user access to cloud services and third-party applications while reducing the administrative overhead of managing direct trust relationships.

Kerberos excels in environments where fast, mutual authentication is required at the protocol level, such as securing SMB file shares, LDAP services, or enterprise application servers. Its ticket-based model reduces the need for frequent password prompts and supports delegation scenarios where services act on behalf of users. However, Kerberos is tightly coupled to the availability and security of the KDC. If the KDC becomes unavailable, users and services may be unable to obtain tickets, leading to authentication failures. OAuth and OpenID Connect distribute this risk by leveraging decentralized token-based systems, often hosted by scalable identity platforms with global availability.

Security considerations also differ between Kerberos and modern alternatives. Kerberos' reliance on symmetric keys for tickets and session keys provides strong protection against forgery, but it requires robust key management practices and strict time synchronization across the environment. In contrast, OAuth and OpenID Connect use public-key cryptography to sign tokens and assertions, reducing the reliance on shared secrets between clients and identity providers. However, bearer tokens in OAuth and OpenID Connect lack built-in replay protection, making TLS a critical component for preventing token interception and misuse.

Another area of distinction is interoperability. Kerberos is widely supported within Windows domains, Unix-based systems, and certain enterprise applications, but it is less suited to modern web and API ecosystems. OAuth, OpenID Connect, and SAML were explicitly designed to secure browser-based interactions, RESTful APIs, and mobile applications, making them better aligned with the requirements of digital transformation initiatives. Organizations adopting cloud-native architectures or customer-facing web applications often prioritize these modern protocols for their flexibility and ease of integration with cloud identity providers and third-party services.

Ultimately, the choice between Kerberos and modern alternatives is often dictated by the specific use case. Enterprises running legacy systems, on-premises applications, or private networks will continue to rely on Kerberos for its efficiency and security within internal environments. Meanwhile, organizations adopting cloud platforms, SaaS applications, and distributed workforces are increasingly turning to OAuth, OpenID Connect, and SAML to enable secure and scalable identity federation.

In many environments, Kerberos and modern alternatives coexist. Hybrid identity models often combine Kerberos for securing internal services with federated protocols such as SAML or OpenID Connect for external access to cloud-based applications. By integrating Kerberos with identity federation tools or cloud-based identity providers, organizations can bridge the gap between traditional authentication models and modern identity frameworks, delivering seamless Single Sign-On experiences across both legacy and cloud-native platforms. As enterprises continue to modernize their IT infrastructure, understanding the strengths and limitations of Kerberos relative to newer protocols will remain essential for building resilient, flexible, and secure authentication ecosystems.

# Case Studies: Kerberos in Large Enterprises

Kerberos has long been a critical component in securing authentication for large enterprises due to its efficiency, scalability, and robustness in distributed environments. Its ability to provide mutual authentication, strong encryption, and Single Sign-On functionality has made it the protocol of choice for organizations with complex infrastructures and thousands of users and devices. Examining real-world case studies of Kerberos implementation in large enterprises highlights both the strengths of the protocol and the challenges organizations face in deploying, managing, and securing it at scale.

One prominent case is a multinational financial institution that operates across more than 50 countries with over 100,000 employees. The institution relies heavily on Kerberos for internal authentication within its global data centers and corporate offices. The organization's Active Directory environment, spanning multiple forests and domains, utilizes Kerberos to secure access to file servers, databases, and internal applications. Kerberos provides seamless Single Sign-On for employees, enabling them to log in once at the start of their workday and access all necessary systems without repeated credential prompts. The institution's security team has implemented cross-realm trusts between different domains to allow seamless authentication across regions while ensuring that ticket issuance is tightly controlled by local Key Distribution Centers to reduce latency and improve performance.

In this deployment, Kerberos plays a key role in securing sensitive financial applications and regulatory systems. Service Principal Names are meticulously managed to avoid duplication and misconfiguration, which could otherwise disrupt critical services. The institution enforces strict delegation controls, utilizing resource-based constrained delegation to limit the ability of services to act on behalf of users only to predefined backend services. To further secure its Kerberos environment, the institution rotates its krbtgt account passwords regularly, enforces AES-256 encryption for all tickets, and integrates Kerberos telemetry into its centralized SIEM system for proactive anomaly detection.

A different example comes from a global manufacturing company with tens of thousands of employees and multiple production plants worldwide. The organization leverages Kerberos in both its IT and Operational Technology (OT) environments to secure access to enterprise resource planning systems, plant control systems, and product lifecycle management platforms. Given the highly sensitive nature of industrial control systems, the organization has implemented Kerberos mutual authentication between clients and backend OT systems to prevent man-in-the-middle attacks and ensure that only trusted endpoints and users can access critical manufacturing resources.

To support Kerberos in remote plants and reduce the dependency on WAN links to central data centers, the company has deployed regional domain controllers and localized KDCs in each production facility. This distributed architecture minimizes ticket acquisition latency and ensures that authentication can continue even during network disruptions. Kerberos service tickets are used to authenticate automated production systems and engineering workstations to backend services, allowing for secure and uninterrupted plant operations. The company also integrates Kerberos with smart card-based multi-factor authentication, requiring engineers and plant operators to use smart cards for initial Kerberos ticket requests, significantly strengthening security in these mission-critical environments.

Another case involves a large government agency with highly classified systems and a complex multi-realm Kerberos environment. The agency's IT infrastructure spans secure enclaves, air-gapped networks, and compartmentalized systems where trust relationships are carefully managed. Kerberos is used extensively to enforce strict authentication policies, with dedicated realms for different security zones and cross-realm trust relationships carefully configured to limit access between zones. The agency implements Kerberos PKINIT (Public Key Cryptography for Initial Authentication in Kerberos) to replace password-based authentication with certificate-based smart card logins, aligning with national security standards and reducing the risk of password-based attacks.

In this environment, Kerberos delegation is tightly controlled to prevent lateral movement between secure systems. Only a handful of authorized services are permitted to delegate user credentials, and constrained delegation is enforced to ensure that credentials are only forwarded to explicitly authorized backend services. Additionally, the agency has deployed hardware security modules to protect the keys associated with its KDCs and to offload cryptographic operations, further hardening its Kerberos infrastructure against advanced threats.

A technology company operating large-scale data centers and providing cloud services to millions of customers also relies on Kerberos to secure its internal infrastructure. In this scenario, Kerberos is used to authenticate service-to-service communications between microservices running within the company's private cloud platform. Containerized applications running in Kubernetes clusters utilize

Kerberos to securely communicate with APIs, databases, and file shares. The company has automated the distribution of Kerberos keytab files to application pods and implements short-lived service tickets to limit the impact of potential credential exposure within its ephemeral containerized workloads.

This organization integrates Kerberos with its service mesh, allowing mutual authentication between services using Kerberos tickets. The use of Kerberos within the service mesh provides an additional layer of security beyond network segmentation, ensuring that only services presenting valid Kerberos tickets can communicate with protected APIs and backend services. To enhance visibility, Kerberos ticket exchanges are logged and monitored through cloud-native monitoring tools, providing real-time insight into authentication flows across thousands of microservices.

A common theme across these case studies is the importance of careful planning, monitoring, and policy enforcement when deploying Kerberos in large enterprises. Each organization faces unique challenges depending on its operational model, regulatory environment, and technology stack, but all rely on Kerberos' ability to provide efficient, scalable, and secure authentication. The ability of Kerberos to integrate with existing infrastructure while supporting strong encryption, mutual authentication, and Single Sign-On continues to make it a trusted choice for securing modern enterprise environments, from financial systems and manufacturing plants to classified government networks and large-scale cloud platforms.

These case studies also demonstrate the increasing need for Kerberos to evolve alongside modern security practices. Enterprises are combining Kerberos with Zero Trust principles, advanced monitoring systems, and identity federation models to ensure that their authentication workflows are resilient, compliant, and ready to meet the demands of complex and distributed IT ecosystems.

# Kerberos Compliance and Regulatory Considerations

Kerberos plays a significant role in securing enterprise authentication workflows, but its implementation must align with an organization's compliance obligations and regulatory frameworks. As enterprises operate in increasingly complex environments governed by diverse and stringent regulatory standards, Kerberos deployments must meet specific security, data protection, and auditing requirements. Whether an organization is subject to industry-specific regulations such as HIPAA, PCI DSS, SOX, or broader data protection laws like the General Data Protection Regulation, the design and operation of Kerberos-based authentication systems must be carefully evaluated to ensure full compliance and mitigate legal or financial risks.

One of the primary compliance considerations related to Kerberos is the protection of authentication credentials and keys. Many regulatory frameworks require organizations to safeguard sensitive data and credentials against unauthorized access. In Kerberos environments, this includes ensuring that secret keys such as the krbtgt account password, service account passwords, and keytab files are securely stored and rotated regularly. For example, PCI DSS mandates the use of strong cryptography and secure key management practices to protect account authentication information. In Kerberos, this translates to enforcing modern encryption algorithms, such as AES-256, for tickets and session keys and disabling weak encryption types like DES or RC4.

The confidentiality and integrity of authentication data in transit are also critical for regulatory compliance. Kerberos inherently provides encryption for tickets and session keys, but it still depends on secure network configurations to prevent interception and replay attacks. Regulators often require organizations to implement strong transport layer security measures, and while Kerberos operates independently of TLS, administrators must ensure that network segments handling Kerberos traffic are hardened against threats. Firewalls, intrusion detection systems, and network segmentation must be configured to limit exposure of Kerberos ports, such as TCP/UDP 88, and to reduce the risk of unauthorized access to authentication traffic.

Logging and auditing are essential components of compliance frameworks and directly impact how Kerberos environments are managed. Regulations such as SOX and HIPAA require that access to sensitive systems is logged and that organizations maintain detailed audit trails of authentication events. Kerberos generates valuable logs related to ticket issuance, service ticket usage, authentication failures, and delegation events. To meet compliance requirements, organizations must ensure that Kerberos logs are retained securely, protected from tampering, and available for forensic investigation if necessary. Security teams should configure centralized logging platforms, such as SIEM systems, to collect and analyze Kerberos events, enabling rapid detection of anomalous behavior, such as unauthorized ticket usage or unusual delegation patterns.

Regulatory bodies also emphasize access control and the principle of least privilege, both of which have direct implications for Kerberos ticketing and delegation configurations. In environments where Kerberos is used to secure access to financial data, health records, or payment processing systems, it is crucial to enforce strict delegation policies. Unconstrained delegation should be avoided, as it can enable services to impersonate users across the network, increasing the risk of privilege escalation. Instead, organizations should adopt constrained or resource-based constrained delegation to limit how and where credentials can be delegated. Doing so helps ensure that access is only granted to users and services with a legitimate business need, in line with regulatory expectations.

Another key consideration is user identity verification during Kerberos authentication. Regulations like HIPAA and PCI DSS stress the importance of strong, multifactor authentication (MFA) for access to systems processing sensitive data. While Kerberos by itself is a single-factor authentication protocol, it can be extended with PKINIT to enable certificate-based smart card logon, aligning with multifactor authentication mandates. Integrating Kerberos with additional identity assurance mechanisms ensures that regulatory requirements for strong authentication are met, reducing the risk of credential-based attacks and demonstrating compliance during audits.

The handling of cross-realm authentication introduces further compliance considerations, particularly in multi-organization or federated environments. When Kerberos realms establish trust relationships, organizations must verify that identity verification standards are consistent across realms and that shared authentication data is protected during transit. Data protection laws like GDPR require organizations to ensure that personal data, including authentication records and identity assertions, are handled securely and are not unnecessarily exposed to third parties. Kerberos administrators must carefully manage cross-realm trust configurations, audit realm policies, and verify that each participating domain adheres to equivalent security and privacy controls.

Data retention and disposal policies are another important aspect of regulatory compliance. Many frameworks require organizations to retain authentication records for a specified period while also mandating the secure deletion of expired records when no longer needed. Kerberos logs, including ticket issuance and service access records, must be managed in accordance with these data retention policies. Automation tools and log management platforms can assist in enforcing retention schedules, ensuring that records are retained for audit purposes but not stored indefinitely in violation of data minimization principles.

In some sectors, regulators also require organizations to demonstrate that authentication systems can support incident response and recovery processes. In the context of Kerberos, this means having documented procedures for responding to authentication-related security incidents, such as Pass-the-Ticket attacks, Golden Ticket forgeries, or unauthorized delegation abuses. Organizations should regularly test their incident response processes, including the ability to revoke or rotate Kerberos keys quickly, disable compromised service accounts, and analyze authentication logs for root cause investigation. Effective incident response capabilities not only strengthen security posture but also demonstrate to regulators that the organization can respond appropriately to breaches or security violations.

Finally, regulatory compliance often mandates regular security assessments and audits of authentication systems. Organizations should schedule periodic internal and external audits of their Kerberos environment to identify misconfigurations, detect vulnerabilities, and verify adherence to policy requirements. Security assessments may include reviewing SPN configurations to prevent spoofing risks, validating encryption policies, ensuring krbtgt key rotations occur at regular intervals, and testing delegation configurations to confirm that least-privilege access is enforced. Findings from these audits should be documented, with corrective actions tracked and implemented as part of a broader compliance and risk management strategy.

As regulatory frameworks continue to evolve and expand, Kerberos deployments must adapt to meet increasingly stringent requirements for security, transparency, and accountability. By aligning Kerberos implementations with best practices in encryption, access control, logging, identity verification, and incident response, organizations can confidently demonstrate compliance while leveraging the protocol's strengths to secure enterprise authentication workflows. The intersection of Kerberos and regulatory compliance highlights the importance of security governance, proactive risk management, and continuous monitoring in protecting sensitive data and maintaining trust in enterprise authentication systems.

# The Future of Kerberos in Enterprise Networks

The future of Kerberos in enterprise networks is being shaped by the evolution of IT infrastructure, emerging security paradigms, and the growing demands of cloud adoption and hybrid architectures. While Kerberos has been a cornerstone of network authentication for decades, the landscape in which it operates is undergoing profound changes. Organizations are moving toward distributed systems, adopting Zero Trust models, and blending traditional on-premises resources with cloud-based platforms. In this shifting environment, Kerberos is evolving to remain relevant and effective, expanding its capabilities while addressing new challenges introduced by modern computing.

Kerberos will continue to serve as a trusted authentication protocol within internal enterprise networks, particularly in environments with large numbers of domain-joined devices and legacy applications that rely on its ticket-based system. In large-scale organizations where Active Directory remains central to identity and access management, Kerberos will still be a critical component for securing file servers, databases, and internal applications. Its efficiency in providing Single Sign-On within well-defined security boundaries will preserve its role in traditional data centers and office networks, where mutual authentication and encryption of ticket exchanges remain critical for protecting against internal threats.

However, as enterprises increasingly adopt cloud services, the role of Kerberos will expand to support hybrid environments that bridge on-premises systems with public and private cloud platforms. Many enterprises are leveraging Azure Active Directory, Google Cloud Identity, or AWS Directory Service alongside their traditional Active Directory domains. As a result, Kerberos is being integrated with identity federation services, enabling organizations to map Kerberos-based identities and authentication flows into cloud-native identity providers. This hybrid model ensures that users can leverage Kerberos-based Single Sign-On for legacy applications while accessing SaaS applications and cloud-hosted workloads through federated authentication protocols such as SAML and OpenID Connect.

Another key development shaping the future of Kerberos is its alignment with Zero Trust security architectures. In a Zero Trust model, network location is no longer a sufficient basis for trust, and all access requests are subject to continuous verification based on identity, device posture, and contextual risk factors. Kerberos, traditionally designed for perimeter-based trust models, is being adapted to fit within this framework. Shorter ticket lifetimes, frequent ticket renewals, and integration with conditional access policies are becoming more common in Kerberos deployments, reducing the duration of implicit trust and ensuring that authentication decisions are dynamically evaluated based on current threat intelligence and risk assessments.

The intersection of Kerberos with PKI (Public Key Infrastructure) will also play a significant role in its future. As organizations look for ways to strengthen identity verification and reduce reliance on passwords, PKINIT (Public Key Cryptography for Initial Authentication in Kerberos) will see broader adoption. PKINIT allows users and services to authenticate using digital certificates and private keys instead of shared secrets, supporting stronger multi-factor authentication mechanisms such as smart cards or hardware security tokens. This shift is aligned with regulatory trends and industry best practices that increasingly mandate the use of multi-factor authentication for access to sensitive systems and data.

Kerberos is also expected to evolve in response to the widespread adoption of containerization, microservices, and serverless architectures. Modern application environments, built on platforms like Kubernetes and cloud-native orchestration tools, require authentication mechanisms that can scale dynamically and operate efficiently within ephemeral workloads. As a result, there is growing interest in optimizing Kerberos ticket issuance and cache handling for containerized applications. Automation of keytab file distribution, tighter integration with service meshes, and improved support for ephemeral service principals will enable Kerberos to serve as a viable authentication mechanism in highly dynamic microservices environments.

In terms of security enhancements, Kerberos will continue to incorporate improvements that address emerging threats. Increased adoption of encryption algorithms such as AES-256 and the eventual introduction of quantum-resistant cryptographic primitives will future-proof Kerberos against advanced cryptanalytic techniques. The ongoing deprecation of legacy encryption methods, combined with efforts to reduce dependency on vulnerable protocols like NTLM, will position Kerberos as a resilient core component of secure identity infrastructures. Additionally, enhanced delegation controls, improved mutual authentication mechanisms, and stricter enforcement of secure ticket exchange protocols will help mitigate the risk of common attack vectors such as Golden Ticket and Silver Ticket attacks.

Machine learning and artificial intelligence will also influence how Kerberos is secured and monitored in the future. The ability to detect anomalous authentication patterns, such as unexpected ticket requests or abnormal service-to-service communications, will become essential for organizations seeking to identify credential-based attacks early. Integration of Kerberos telemetry into AI-driven security platforms will enable more effective threat detection and incident response, helping enterprises respond to rapidly evolving attack tactics.

The rise of edge computing and IoT will also impact Kerberos deployments. As more organizations deploy services and devices outside traditional data center environments, there will be a need for lightweight Kerberos clients that can operate in resource-constrained or distributed edge locations. The protocol's ticket-based model offers advantages in intermittent connectivity scenarios, where devices may not have persistent access to a central authentication authority. This will likely drive the development of optimized Kerberos implementations tailored for edge and IoT environments.

Lastly, as enterprises modernize their identity and access management strategies, Kerberos will continue to coexist with other authentication protocols. Organizations will adopt hybrid models where Kerberos secures internal systems while federated protocols like OAuth 2.0 and SAML provide authentication for cloud-hosted applications and external services. Identity federation platforms will serve as bridges, translating Kerberos-based credentials into token-based authentication mechanisms that are more suitable for modern web and API-driven ecosystems. This interoperability will allow organizations to leverage the strengths of Kerberos within the boundaries of their internal networks while extending access securely to external environments.

Kerberos is poised to remain an integral part of enterprise security for the foreseeable future, evolving alongside new technologies and adapting to emerging security paradigms. Its ability to provide mutual authentication, strong encryption, and seamless Single Sign-On will continue to deliver value in enterprise environments, even as those environments become more distributed, cloud-integrated, and dynamic. The continued development of Kerberos, combined with best practices in deployment and monitoring, will ensure that it remains a critical component of secure and adaptable enterprise authentication strategies.

# Conclusion and Best Practices for Kerberos Security

Kerberos remains one of the most robust and widely deployed authentication protocols in enterprise environments, offering mutual authentication, ticket-based access control, and encryption for securing user and service identities. Its design, rooted in a symmetric key model and a trusted Key Distribution Center, has proven highly effective for internal networks where efficiency, reliability, and centralized control are paramount. However, as enterprise architectures have expanded to encompass hybrid cloud environments, remote workforces, and increasingly complex threat landscapes, organizations must apply a combination of modern security best practices and careful system design to maintain the integrity and security of their Kerberos deployments.

One of the most essential best practices for securing Kerberos systems is ensuring proper key management, particularly for highly sensitive accounts such as the krbtgt account. The krbtgt account acts as the foundation of trust for issuing Ticket Granting Tickets, and its compromise can allow attackers to forge tickets across the entire Kerberos realm. Organizations should enforce regular rotation of the krbtgt account password, using long and complex values to minimize the risk of offline attacks. Password rotation schedules should be clearly documented, and administrators should coordinate key updates carefully to avoid disruptions to ticket issuance and validation across domain controllers.

Service Principal Names should be closely audited and managed to avoid duplication, conflicts, or misconfigurations. SPNs are essential for identifying services to the Key Distribution Center, and improper registration can result in authentication failures or potential spoofing attacks. Administrators should periodically inventory all SPNs registered within the environment, ensuring that each is assigned to the correct service account and conforms to naming conventions that reduce the risk of human error. Additionally, it is important to avoid associating SPNs with user accounts whenever possible, as this practice can increase the attack surface for Kerberoasting attacks.

Enforcing the use of modern encryption standards is equally critical. Organizations should disable legacy encryption types such as DES and RC4 across their Kerberos realms, mandating the exclusive use of AES-128 or AES-256 encryption for ticket and session key exchanges. This hardening step not only improves resistance to cryptographic attacks but also aligns with industry standards such as NIST guidelines and PCI DSS requirements. Clients and services must be configured to support these modern algorithms, and administrators should validate encryption settings on both Kerberos clients and domain controllers.

Delegation policies must also be configured with precision. Unconstrained delegation introduces significant risk by allowing services to impersonate users to any other resource within the domain, increasing the potential for lateral movement in the event of a service compromise. Organizations should replace unconstrained delegation with constrained or resource-based constrained delegation wherever possible. These more secure delegation models restrict the ability of services to forward user credentials to explicitly authorized backend services, adhering to the principle of least privilege.

Time synchronization is a non-negotiable requirement for Kerberos environments. Because Kerberos relies on timestamps to prevent replay attacks and validate ticket freshness, all clients, servers, and KDCs must be synchronized using a reliable Network Time Protocol source. Organizations should configure their infrastructure to synchronize time regularly and ensure fallback mechanisms are in place to maintain synchronization during service outages. Consistent timekeeping prevents unnecessary ticket rejections and guards against certain classes of replay and spoofing attacks.

Monitoring and logging are integral to maintaining Kerberos security. Administrators should configure domain controllers and Kerberos clients to log all relevant authentication events, including ticket issuance, renewals, pre-authentication failures, and service ticket usage. These logs should be forwarded to a centralized SIEM platform, where they can be analyzed for indicators of compromise such as Pass-the-Ticket attacks, Golden Ticket forgeries, and abnormal ticket usage patterns. Security teams should establish alerting rules for events such as tickets with anomalously long lifetimes, service ticket requests from unexpected sources, or repeated authentication failures targeting service accounts.

Strengthening Kerberos security also involves integrating multifactor authentication into the initial ticket issuance process. While Kerberos itself is based on single-factor authentication, organizations can implement PKINIT to replace or augment passwords with X.509 certificate-based authentication. This enables smart card logon or other certificate-driven MFA workflows, reducing reliance on static passwords and improving resistance to credential theft.

Another important best practice is the segmentation of Kerberos realms to limit trust boundaries. In large enterprises, it is advisable to establish distinct Kerberos realms or Active Directory domains for separate business units, regions, or security zones. Cross-realm trusts should be configured sparingly and only after assessing the security posture of all participating realms. By limiting transitive trust relationships, organizations can reduce the risk that a compromise in one segment will propagate to others.

Incident response preparedness is a key component of Kerberos security. Organizations must have documented and regularly tested procedures for responding to Kerberos-related incidents. This includes the ability to quickly revoke or re-issue keytab files, reset compromised service account passwords, rotate krbtgt keys, and analyze authentication logs for signs of malicious activity. Recovery plans should account for the impact of ticket lifetimes and delegation configurations, ensuring that credentials are invalidated swiftly during an incident.

Training and awareness for system administrators and security teams play a crucial role in maintaining Kerberos security. Administrators must be well-versed in the nuances of Kerberos ticketing, SPN registration, delegation settings, and encryption policy enforcement. Regular security reviews, penetration testing, and red teaming exercises help organizations identify weaknesses and validate the effectiveness of their Kerberos security posture.

Finally, Kerberos must be integrated thoughtfully within hybrid and cloud environments. In modern enterprise architectures, Kerberos often coexists with identity federation platforms and cloud-native authentication protocols such as OAuth 2.0 and OpenID Connect. Organizations should design workflows that bridge Kerberos authentication with cloud identity providers securely, ensuring that tickets are translated into tokens in accordance with Zero Trust principles. Hybrid identity models require careful attention to trust boundaries, delegation risks, and encryption settings to maintain the integrity of authentication across cloud and on-premises assets.

Kerberos remains a vital component of enterprise security, but its effectiveness depends on rigorous adherence to best practices. By combining robust technical controls, careful planning, and continuous monitoring, organizations can ensure that Kerberos continues to provide secure, reliable, and efficient authentication in an increasingly complex and distributed IT landscape.

www.ingramcontent.com/pod-product-compliance
Lightning Source LLC
LaVergne TN
LVHW051235050326
832903LV00028B/2411

PKI integration also simplifies cross-realm authentication and federation. In environments with multiple Kerberos realms that must interoperate securely, PKI facilitates the establishment of trust relationships between realms without relying solely on shared keys. By issuing certificates to KDCs in each realm and configuring cross-realm PKINIT support, organizations can create secure authentication bridges, allowing users from one realm to access services in another using certificate-based trust. This is particularly valuable in large federated environments or mergers and acquisitions, where unifying identity infrastructure may take time.

From a technical perspective, enabling PKINIT requires modifying Kerberos configuration files to specify the relevant PKI parameters. In MIT Kerberos, administrators must configure krb5.conf to point to the PKINIT anchor certificate file, define the PKINIT identity for the client, and specify supported encryption types. The KDC's kdc.conf file must also be updated to include the KDC certificate and private key, and to enforce PKINIT requirements for specific client principals or globally across the realm. Similarly, Active Directory-based Kerberos implementations automatically support PKINIT when integrated with Windows Certificate Services and Group Policy configurations for smart card logon.

While PKI enhances Kerberos authentication, it introduces additional considerations related to certificate lifecycle management. Certificates must be issued, distributed, renewed, and revoked according to organizational policies. Automation tools, such as enterprise certificate management platforms, can streamline these tasks by integrating with directory services and Kerberos infrastructure to ensure certificates remain valid and are rotated before expiration. Failure to properly manage certificates can lead to authentication outages if expired or revoked certificates are used during the PKINIT process.

Performance is another consideration when integrating PKI with Kerberos. The PKINIT process introduces additional computational overhead compared to traditional Kerberos exchanges, as it requires public key operations, certificate validation, and Diffie-Hellman key exchanges. Organizations deploying PKINIT at scale should evaluate the performance capabilities of their KDC infrastructure and consider the corresponding private key during the Authentication Service exchange, establishing a secure session without relying on shared secrets. This approach aligns with enterprise security policies that favor certificate-based authentication and supports strong, multi-factor authentication mechanisms such as smart cards.

Integrating PKI with Kerberos via PKINIT significantly enhances security by mitigating risks associated with password-based authentication. Passwords, even when combined with pre-authentication mechanisms, are susceptible to brute-force, phishing, and credential theft attacks. By replacing or augmenting passwords with certificates protected by hardware devices like smart cards or USB tokens, organizations can enforce higher assurance levels and meet regulatory compliance requirements. PKINIT also introduces Perfect Forward Secrecy, as session keys are negotiated using ephemeral Diffie-Hellman keys, ensuring that compromising long-term keys does not retroactively expose past session data.

The process of integrating PKI with Kerberos typically starts with the deployment of a trusted certificate authority that issues certificates to users and systems. The Key Distribution Center must also possess a valid certificate signed by a CA that is trusted by the clients. The KDC certificate is used to establish a mutual trust relationship with clients during the PKINIT exchange. Both the KDC and the clients perform certificate validation, ensuring that certificates are properly signed, have not expired, and are not listed on a Certificate Revocation List or invalidated through Online Certificate Status Protocol checks.

Kerberos environments that integrate with PKI often use smart card logon as a common authentication method. In this scenario, users insert their smart card into a reader, and the operating system initiates the Kerberos PKINIT process using the certificate and private key stored on the smart card. The result is a seamless Single Sign-On experience where the user authenticates once and obtains a Ticket Granting Ticket, which is then used to access services throughout the network without further credential prompts. Smart card logon is widely adopted in government, military, and financial sectors, where strict identity verification standards are enforced.

Finally, once the upgrade or migration is completed, administrators should monitor the environment closely to identify and resolve any lingering authentication issues. Integrating the upgraded Kerberos infrastructure with Security Information and Event Management platforms ensures that suspicious activity is detected promptly, while ongoing audits and health checks validate the long-term success of the project.

Upgrading and migrating Kerberos systems is a technically demanding but rewarding initiative that strengthens the security and performance of enterprise authentication workflows. By following a systematic process that includes assessment, planning, testing, and post-deployment validation, organizations can successfully modernize their Kerberos infrastructure and align it with contemporary security and operational best practices.

# Kerberos and PKI Integration

Kerberos and Public Key Infrastructure integration provides a robust security framework by combining the benefits of symmetric key cryptography with the scalability and flexibility of digital certificates. Traditionally, Kerberos has been based on the use of shared secret keys for both client and service authentication. While highly efficient, this model has limitations, especially in environments where managing large numbers of keys and identities can become operationally complex. Integrating PKI into Kerberos addresses these challenges by allowing authentication workflows to incorporate digital certificates, enhancing security, simplifying key management, and supporting additional use cases such as smart card logon and secure communications across organizational boundaries.

One of the most common implementations of Kerberos and PKI integration is the use of Public Key Cryptography for Initial Authentication in Kerberos, commonly referred to as PKINIT. PKINIT extends the standard Kerberos protocol by enabling clients to use X.509 certificates instead of passwords when requesting an initial Ticket Granting Ticket from the Key Distribution Center. In this model, clients present their digital certificate and prove possession of migration. During this process, care must be taken to synchronize DNS records and verify that client machines resolve hostnames correctly to avoid SPN mismatches.

Client reconfiguration is another key step in the migration process. Kerberos clients need updated krb5.conf files or equivalent settings to recognize and trust the target KDC servers and realms. On Linux and Unix systems using MIT Kerberos or Heimdal, this often involves updating the realm and KDC sections of the configuration file. In Active Directory environments, Group Policy settings can be used to direct Windows clients to the appropriate domain controllers acting as KDCs. Any services relying on Kerberos, such as web servers, databases, and file servers, must also be reconfigured to accept tickets from the new realm.

Security hardening should accompany any Kerberos upgrade or migration. This includes enforcing strong ticket policies, such as limiting ticket lifetimes, enabling pre-authentication, and configuring delegation settings to minimize attack surfaces. Additionally, new features available in upgraded Kerberos versions, such as FAST (Flexible Authentication Secure Tunneling), should be evaluated and implemented where appropriate to further enhance protection against credential-based attacks.

Testing is crucial during both upgrades and migrations. Administrators should validate that clients can successfully request and use Ticket Granting Tickets and service tickets from the target KDC. Service-to-service authentication flows should be thoroughly tested, especially for applications that depend on constrained or resource-based constrained delegation. Log files from both clients and KDCs should be reviewed for errors or anomalies, and performance metrics should be collected to compare pre- and post-migration authentication latencies.

Communication and change management play an important role in the success of Kerberos transitions. Users should be informed of any changes that may affect their login experience or access to networked services, especially if client-side reconfiguration or new credential issuance is required. Change control processes should include rollback plans in case of unforeseen issues during or after the transition.